AI For Business

A practical guide for business leaders to extract value from Artificial Intelligence

Peter Verster

Rethink

First published in Great Britain in 2024
by Rethink Press (www.rethinkpress.com)

© Copyright Peter Verster

All rights reserved. No part of this publication may be reproduced, stored in or introduced into a retrieval system, or transmitted, in any form, or by any means (electronic, mechanical, photocopying, recording or otherwise) without the prior written permission of the publisher.

The right of Peter Verster to be identified as the author of this work has been asserted by him in accordance with the Copyright, Designs and Patents Act 1988.

This book is sold subject to the condition that it shall not, by way of trade or otherwise, be lent, resold, hired out, or otherwise circulated without the publisher's prior consent in any form of binding or cover other than that in which it is published and without a similar condition including this condition being imposed on the subsequent purchaser.

Contents

Introduction	1
The AI revolution	2
How this book can help	4
Summary	7
1 Introduction To AI	9
The impact of AI on businesses	10
Talent is the secret ingredient	15
AI and job creation	17
Summary	19
2 Understanding AI	21
The definition of AI: Past, present and future	21
Key types of AI	26
The power of AI: Real-world case studies	32
Summary	41

3	**The AI Landscape**	**43**
	Surveying the AI ecosystem	43
	Sector-specific implications of AI	46
	Global trends in approaching AI	56
	Summary	63
4	**Preparing Your Organisation For AI**	**65**
	Identifying AI opportunities	66
	Core AI principles	68
	Strategy	75
	Cultivating AI skills within your organisation	78
	Navigating moral, legal and societal challenges	85
	Summary	88
5	**Achieving Competitive Advantage Through AI**	**89**
	Your roadmap to implementing AI	90
	Building data infrastructure	98
	Three categories of AI initiatives	101
	Measuring and monitoring progress	108
	Summary	111
6	**Overcoming Challenges And Mitigating Risks**	**113**
	Cultural, technical and regulatory hurdles	113
	Ensuring data privacy and security	119

	Fairness concerns and mitigating bias	122
	Summary	128
7	**The Future Of AI In Organisations**	**131**
	The next frontier of AI in business	132
	Maintaining your competitive edge	140
	Preparing for disruptions	143
	Summary	147
Conclusion		**149**
	Recap of key takeaways	150
	Final thoughts on embracing AI for competitive advantage	154
	Summary	159
Notes		**161**
Acknowledgements		**167**
The Author		**169**

Introduction

In ancient Greek mythology, Prometheus, the god of fire, was prized for his intellect and creativity. It was Prometheus who moulded man out of clay. Zeus, king of the gods, forbade Prometheus from giving humans fire for fear of what they would become and the godlike power they would wield with the ability to invent, innovate and create that such a tool would give them.

Disobeying Zeus, Prometheus, humankind's greatest champion, stole fire from the gods and gave it to his beloved creation. It enabled humans to thrive – to cook their food, heat their homes, make tools and create an economy. In short, it allowed them to build civilisation and leave behind their dependence on the gods.

Enraged, Zeus decided to punish humankind by creating a mortal of perfect beauty, Pandora. Zeus gave her a jar, which she was forbidden to open, and sent her to live among humans. Eventually, her curiosity got the better of her and when she opened the jar, she released all the evils it contained into the world. When she finally managed to get the lid back on the jar, the only thing left inside was hope.

These two intertwined tales each contain their own cautionary lessons, which are still relevant as we move into a future with artificial intelligence (AI). Undoubtedly, AI has the ability to transform the world as we know it. It could create, solve, innovate, iterate – it could be the tool with which we forge the newest form of our civilisation. Of course, we could also be giving sentience to something that might eventually outstrip us, opening the lid on a jar of mayhem. It's up to us to decide how we will use the incredible opportunities being presented to us.

The AI revolution

In a world teetering on the precipice of a digital evolution, the infusion of AI into business has become one of the defining conversations for the future of enterprise. When I set out to write this book, I was aware that there was a growing interest in the use of AI in business. Inspired by big players in the digital space, more and more companies were identifying the potential of

AI to do things like streamline their operations, find new sources of revenue and make their teams more productive. There was, however, still uncertainty around the ways AI could help and the ways it could be applied across different industries.

Then, as I set about my research for the book, there was a sudden, almost cataclysmic, shift in the market. What changed? Well, put simply, ChatGPT launched itself onto the scene and, seemingly overnight, what had been exploratory conversations about innovative new ways of working had become the zeitgeist. The paradigm had shifted. AI was no longer a question of 'if', it was now just 'how'.

At this pivotal juncture, businesses find themselves in the process of a metamorphosis driven by technology. The AI revolution, ever evolving, has permeated organisational structures, compelling leaders to redefine their business models. AI's relentless expansion, coupled with the competitive ethos of the modern business landscape, necessitates an understanding of and an astute approach to AI integration. The influx of AI innovations has led to an expectation overflow in the market, and this book is intended to be a way of exploring the dynamics of AI to prepare organisations to meet, if not exceed, these growing expectations.

AI represents a paradigm shift – a new lens through which we can view the way we do business, the way we run our organisations, and the way we interact with our colleagues and customers. Properly understood and used to its full extent, AI sits as part of a transformation journey that will impact business models, customer expectations, competitive advantage and talent acquisition as well as our products and processes. Being open and ready for this kind of strategy shift will be the difference between simply using AI and being a digitally driven organisation.

Businesses are moving into a reality where customer orientation is merging with technological innovation. We're moving towards a point where organisational success is dependent on AI. The constant flux in global trends and AI applications and the variety of approaches to AI between different countries means it is imperative to comprehend the global AI landscape.

How this book can help

This book – a synthesis of deep research and practical wisdom – offers a pragmatic perspective and serves as a guide for business leaders navigating the uncharted waters of AI implementation. Studying AI at the University of Oxford and with a background in digital transformation, I've attempted to unravel the myriad dimensions of AI to present a comprehensive reference book to support leaders in leveraging AI for business enhancement.

INTRODUCTION

As AI infiltrates various sectors from healthcare to retail, understanding its sector-specific implications is imperative for leaders who want to take all the potential of AI and tailor it to their own context. Using an approach balanced between strategic insight and actionable knowledge, I will guide leaders through the process of identifying AI opportunities, developing an integrated AI strategy, and fostering an environment conducive to AI. With the war for talent intensifying, I offer insight into how to cultivate AI skills within your organisation and create an employee value proposition (EVP) that aligns with the twenty-first-century skills required to position yourself strategically in a globalised, AI-driven world.

I'll begin with some context around AI and where it fits into the narrative of enterprise and business growth. We often tend to view AI as a tool to add to a myriad of other tools we use in our organisations, but there's a bigger picture I want to be sure isn't ignored as I focus on the practical application of these technologies.

Next, I'll provide a short explanation of AI and its key types, exploring how businesses are making use of them to improve customer service, streamline processes and increase profits. I'll break these down to help you work out which AI opportunities may work for your organisation.

I'll move on to use cases that have led to business transformations across different sectors. I'll offer some examples of the impact AI can have across business functions and sectors. Then I'll present you with a practical guide for assessing your readiness for AI and cultivating the right talent to support your digital ambitions. AI implementation isn't as simple as just bringing tools into your business. One of the main reasons for the failure of digital transformation projects is the lack of preparation across the organisation. This book will help you to ask the right questions to assess your company's readiness for AI initiatives and build a coherent and well-structured roadmap for implementation that achieves competitive advantage and ensures you get the maximum value from your transformation journey.

The book delves into the core AI principles – agility, trust, customer orientation, and innovation – to assess an organisation's readiness for AI. Combining these principles will help businesses to remain relevant and resilient in a world underpinned by AI. By addressing cultural, technical and regulatory hurdles, I will equip leaders with the knowledge to mitigate challenges and risks inherent in AI adoption.

There are, undoubtedly, a number of moral, legal and societal challenges that organisations must navigate. Ethical considerations and responsible AI have emerged as cornerstones in the discussion surrounding AI implementations. I'll identify this ethical labyrinth, addressing concerns related to AI bias, data collection, and governance. Going beyond the surface,

I'll help leaders build responsible AI, ensuring data privacy and security and fostering fairness and transparency in AI applications.

I'll outline the value engineering process, from deciding on AI initiatives to developing the benefits case, building data infrastructure and measuring and monitoring progress. You'll learn to leverage AI for operational efficiency, enhance customer experience and personalisation, and transform data into actionable insights for informed decision-making.

Finally, I'll address the future of AI for enterprise, exploring the upcoming trends and the next frontier and focusing on the democratisation of AI, hyperautomated processes and human–AI collaboration. I'll provide insight into maintaining a competitive edge with a long-term AI strategy and preparing for future disruptions by fostering agility and resilience in an AI era.

Summary

This book is a tool – a guide for leaders who know that AI is the future for business growth and efficiency but are unsure on how to get started or how to ensure long-term success. It will act as a catalyst in empowering business leaders to embrace AI with strategic discernment and ethical responsibility. I'll demystify the complexities of AI, offering business owners a tangible blueprint to traverse the landscape. At this current moment in time, this guide has particular relevance and use, as it bridges the gap between AI potential and organisational transformation. By fostering a holistic understanding and delivering practical insights, I offer it as a valuable tool to sculpt a future where combining AI and human ingenuity redefines the contours of business excellence.

ONE
Introduction To AI

This opening chapter will lay the foundation of my exploration by introducing AI's core concepts, and discussing the many ways it is likely to impact on businesses in the coming years and how it is reshaping the global commercial landscape. I'll reflect on the crucial aspect of business models, analysing how the assimilation of AI necessitates a reimagining and reinvention of existing structures, and delve into how businesses can navigate this overflow by strategically aligning their AI capabilities to not just meet but exceed these expectations. I'll talk about the too-often-missed element of successful AI projects – the talent on the ground – and finish by considering the potential of AI to create jobs.

The impact of AI on businesses

It feels like AI has burst into our lives in an extraordinarily rapid way. Technologies that could once only be imagined are becoming reality in front of our eyes. AI has become the zeitgeist, the conversation of the moment. In response, many leaders are looking for ways to incorporate AI and machine learning (ML) into their businesses to enhance their productivity and give them the competitive edge. With hundreds of new AI applications entering the marketplace on an almost weekly basis, understanding the options and knowing where to start can feel overwhelming.

With an ever-evolving digital landscape lying before us, we're constantly presented with a plethora of choices, each of which we can embrace or eschew. What's clear is that ignoring the shift to digital and the opportunities presented by AI isn't an option for businesses that want to meet the rapidly changing needs and expectations of their customers.

In a digital world, there is a strategic imperative for leaders to enhance their offer in line with major digital players. AI can bring unique and exciting opportunities to engage with customers, meet their needs and create additional value. The two questions allied with this are: how willing are businesses to embrace digital transformation, and how capable are they of implementing AI with the maximum benefit to themselves and their customers?

Your business model

To begin the journey into any digital transformation, you must strip right back to the core of your company – your business model. Business models vary across companies but, in essence, they are the vehicle through which your company creates and delivers value to your customers, employees and partners. They are the mechanism you use to drive profit.

Using your business model as the lens through which to view AI will help identify some of the challenges arising for your business. With rapid advances in technology and digital capability, consumers' ideas of what value means are constantly shifting. Customers – their needs, behaviours and expectations – are changing faster than businesses can keep up with. For consumers, value is becoming more elusive as it evolves beyond the simple definition of 'utility of goods'.

Technological innovation is spreading quickly, impacting the social, cultural and individual contexts that influence the value judgements customers make. What used to be a linear evolution, primarily based on value as determined by price, has turned into an unpredictable environment where goods are the commodities, and value has become a perception based on the experience you give your customers, determined by service outcomes. In short, it's no longer enough to deliver the product. The entire customer journey is now being judged.

What does this mean for your business? What needs to change and in what order? Where should you start? To answer that, you need to look at where your customers place their value and understand their expectations for the way that you operate.

The expectation overflow

'The expectation overflow' is the term used to describe the shift that has taken place in customers' value judgements. In other words, it means the hoops you need to jump through to please your customers. Advancements in technology have enabled digital players to offer a new and better level of service and/or experience to their customers. As customers become used to this, they no longer place value in it. Instead, they come to expect it as normal practice.

Take Amazon Prime's free next-day delivery service. This speed of service has become a societal norm for a large proportion of consumers, meaning their expectation has shifted for all other organisations. Having become accustomed to this level of service, customers now expect it as standard from all companies. Rather than free next-day delivery being seen as a bonus or an added extra – a positive value judgement, the lack of it is seen as a shortcoming – a negative value judgement.

The balance of power has tipped towards the consumer as digital technology has given them more information and choice. Standing out in this global marketplace has become the new concern for those looking to differentiate themselves.

This is where AI comes into play, offering new opportunities to surprise and delight customers and pull away from the competition. Used correctly, it can help you do more to meet the evolving expectations of your customers.

With the digital landscape changing so quickly, companies must not only keep up with the AI tools available and the expectations of their customers, but also navigate the interplay between these two axes. In this paradigm, digital is not the end but the means to deliver the highest-quality customer value proposition (CVP). While this requires a new way of operating based on continuously evolving and understanding what constitutes value in the customer's mind, the reward can be huge. It's the ability to respond more quickly, pivot with the market and explore new revenue streams. It's the ability to capitalise on the opportunities presented by AI, leading to sustained competitive advantage for those who invest in it.

Competitive advantage

With customer expectations at an all-time high, finding areas of advantage over competitors is ever more challenging. This is compounded by the current economic climate in which budgets and profit margins are squeezed. It is worth remembering, however, that it is often in times of economic turbulence that innovation can have the biggest impact. It is exactly in this context that AI is breaking through and bringing value.

While many businesses have already begun to use AI for automation and personalisation, competitive advantage will come from creating business models that put AI and digital innovation at the heart of the organisation as opposed to just implementing individual applications.

At the core of this approach is data collection. Consistent data collection across a business allows AI to process and analyse customer, employee and supplier data, giving rise to multiple opportunities for increased efficiency and effectiveness. Using AI to gain a deeper understanding of individual customer behaviours will allow for better targeting and increased sales. Implementing the same or similar AI to analyse patterns and trends will improve customer demand forecasts, leading to more efficient supply chain management. Using the right AI systems in the right places will be more effective than following the crowd.

Coca-Cola, for example, have transformed their entire business model to support the evolution of AI and its effectiveness across the company. They regularly update their marketing campaigns, incorporating the latest AI technology to increase engagement. In 2018 this included using Augmented Reality, in 2022 they tapped into nonfungible tokens, and in 2023 they were encouraging user-generated content via a new platform that combines ChatGPT-4 and DALL-E to create branded artwork.

In supply chain management, Coca-Cola uses AI to optimise inventory levels and predict demand. This means they have the right amount of their product available in the right place at the right time. They have reduced costs, improved efficiency and, crucially, ensured there's no disruption to the customer experience.

I'll return to data collection and processing in Chapter Five, where I'll give you an overview of how to build a data infrastructure that is reliable, compliant and useful.

Talent is the secret ingredient

I've discussed the impact of AI on the CVP (and there are many studies on digital transformation and the CVP), but what about the importance and potential impact on employees? While most companies have a fair idea of their CVP, many have never given thought to their EVP. This could be a strategic mistake. A 2013 study on innovation conducted by Chalmers University of Technology, using Google as a subject, concluded that the top two factors contributing to Google's success are individual employees followed by employee culture.[1] They attributed both to the talent selection process.

For a company to create an environment in which innovation will thrive, employing the right people is a crucial step. Having a diverse leadership team, for example, will result in a more innovative organisation that is 70% more likely to capture new markets.[2] A study conducted by *Forbes* showed that workplace diversity is the key driver to innovation.[3]

As Steve Forbes has noted, 'The real source of wealth and capital in this era is not material things – it's the human mind, the human spirit, the human imagination, and our faith in the future.'[4] This is a crucial point to remember on your AI journey. AI is not a replacement for human talent. Instead, it's a tool for talented individuals to use to unlock new levels of creativity and productivity.

The foresight to see the potential of AI and the creative ability to realise and use digital innovations at pace will set companies over and above their competitors, but this requires high-performing colleagues to be in the right place to bring the necessary value.

An industry study by McKinsey discovered that high-performing team members are up to 800% more productive than average employees.⁵

On a typical three-year project this would mean that replacing just 20% of average-ability talent with this high-performing talent would see that project completed in one year, getting you to the market up to two years faster than the competition.⁶ Ensuring these employees are properly skilled and equipped to use AI creatively could drive further improvements and operational efficiencies.

AI and job creation

There is widespread concern about AI and automation eliminating jobs. It's fair to say that automation and ML has taken, and will continue to take, low-skilled manual jobs and repetitive work, but AI has brought with it a host of new opportunities. It is quickly showing itself to be one of the fastest job creation tools, expected to create 15 million jobs by 2025.⁷ While many low-skilled and manual tasks have the potential to become automated, there is a growing need for more skilled workers.

The emerging skills needed for the future are becoming clearer by the day. According to LinkedIn's 2022 report on jobs of the future, new job roles that will become more commonplace over the next five years include digital account manager, chief data officer, digital communications manager, design learning manager and social media strategist.[8] These are roles that will support companies to move into the digital space with confidence, build a reputation as knowledge creators, embrace innovation and pivot in response to customer need. Organisations looking to embrace digital transformation are experiencing a gap in the skills that exist within their employee base – a lack of those they most need for digital transformation to be a success.

One of the first things you'll need to assess on your AI journey is the digital literacy of your top-tier management. Creating a digital mindset for your organisation needs to be modelled from the top. Your higher-level managers will need to understand and be on board with your AI goals, and be on hand to support the upskilling and reskilling of their team members.

Alongside this you'll need to analyse your workforce's digital skill set and formulate how best to fill in any gaps. Organisations across all sectors, from logistics and manufacturing through to entertainment and hospitality, are evolving into technology companies that use data to streamline their operations and better meet their customers' needs. The economic necessity to remain globally competitive, irrespective of the market, industry and approach, requires companies to prioritise the acquisition and retention of employees with skills and competencies that contribute directly to the bottom line.

With digital transformation requiring the buy-in and responsiveness of internal stakeholders across an entire organisation, there also needs to be a pro-active approach to upskilling existing talent. I'll address these issues in Chapter Four, where I'll explore how to cultivate digital leaders within your company.

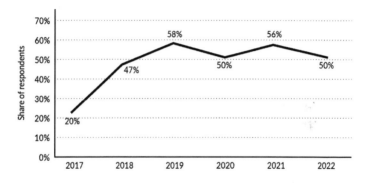

AI adoption rate in businesses globally from 2017 to 2022

Notes: Worldwide, 3–7 May and 15–17 August 2022; 1,492 respondents; participants represented the full range of regions, industries, company sizes, functional specialities and tenures. Source: McKinsey & Company; ID 1368935

Summary

I have begun by looking at the impact AI is already having on businesses, the way consumer expectation has shifted to match the speed of innovation, and the way AI can create competitive advantage for those who use it wisely. I have also looked at the impact of AI on talent and job creation, addressing some of the concerns people have about AI and automation eliminating jobs.

TWO
Understanding AI

In this chapter I'll explore the journey that AI has gone on and consider some definitions and boundaries around what we mean when we talk about AI. I'll specifically talk about ML, Natural Language Processing (NLP) and robotics, as these are three of the most widely used and rapidly developing types of AI. I'll then turn to some real-world case studies and explore current usage for things like automation, data analysis, personalisation, customer support, and supply chain and marketing.

The definition of AI: Past, present and future

In a business landscape that is continuously shifting, the term 'artificial intelligence' sparks an amalgamation of curiosity, apprehension and anticipation.

Five years ago, talk of AI evoked futuristic scenes – either of robots taking over human roles in a dystopian-style setting, or of self-driving cars and drones making our lives smoother. The optimistic among us agree it presents opportunities for unprecedented growth and productivity, though the more cautious might temper that by reminding us of the inherent risks and lack of regulation in place for AI users and developers. Enterprise AI, which provides solutions to specific, high-value, large use cases, is already proving to be a game changer, and in this chapter I'll show you how by looking at some of the innovative ways enterprise AI has been applied. First I'll explore the breadth of AI – its roots and where it might possibly go – and some of the common terminologies you'll see surrounding the AI conversation.

There has been a shift in the way we think about and interact with computing over the past few decades, with digital innovations coming thick and fast since Apple first launched the iPhone in 2007. There has always been a certain amount of fear surrounding AI, what it is and what it might be capable of in the future, but over the past twelve months the acceleration of what ML can do has been eye-opening and, along with a jump in the capabilities of generative AI, there has been an increase in the social acceptance of AI as a part of daily life.

The reason for this is that the foundations of AI have changed. ML used to be built on logic, mathematical equations and coding. For the majority of people it was unintelligible. Those developing the tech then began to realise that for AI to become popular, first it needed to do the things that people do on a day-to-day basis – make the judgement calls and decisions, address the real-world problems – and second it needed to be usable by those who don't have development capabilities. Quite rapidly, AI has become more intuitive and accessible – most generative AI tools have evolved to respond to plain text prompts so anyone can use them, and a massive amount of emphasis and expertise was poured into ML to create generative AI tools that enable people to complete day-to-day tasks more efficiently.

Before I delve deeper, let's take a moment to acknowledge an interesting paradox: although AI feels like a concept of the future, its roots stretch far back into our past. The dream of creating machines that can think and act like humans has been an integral part of our collective imagination since ancient times. Mythologies abound with tales of animated statues and mechanical beings. Philosophers have debated the nature of intelligence and consciousness for millennia. Today's AI is not an abrupt revelation but rather a culmination of these age-old dreams and debates.

Past

AI's formal journey began in the mid-twentieth century, driven by pioneers who believed the human intellect could be emulated by machines. They envisioned a world where machines could play chess, understand natural language and solve mathematical problems. Early AI research was steeped in optimism; however, this enthusiasm met significant hurdles. Despite these challenges, the foundational theories and algorithms crafted during these initial years laid the groundwork for the AI we see today.

Present

Fast-forward to the current epoch, and we find ourselves amid an AI revolution. What changed? In simple terms, it was the confluence of massive data sets, improved algorithms and exponential increases in computing power. Today's AI is not so much about emulating human intelligence as enhancing it. Whether it's a recommendation engine suggesting your next book, an AI-driven diagnostic tool detecting diseases with unparalleled accuracy, or chatbots providing round-the-clock customer support – AI is everywhere.

It's crucial to remember that AI is not a monolithic entity. It's an umbrella term encompassing a range of techniques and methodologies. From ML, where systems learn and improve from experience, to neural networks inspired by our brain's architecture, to NLP that allows machines to understand and generate human language, AI is multifaceted.

For business owners, it's essential to recognise that AI isn't just about automation; it's about augmentation. It's not just about replacing the human workforce but empowering it. Think of AI as a magnifying glass – it can highlight inefficiencies, offer insights and allow your organisation to operate at a scale and speed previously deemed unattainable.

Future

Envisioning the future of AI is like predicting the trajectory of a star – bright and promising, yet intertwined with the unknown. As AI technologies continue to mature, we can anticipate them becoming even more integrated into our daily lives and business operations. We'll see smarter algorithms, enhanced human–AI collaboration, and, potentially, the birth of machines that can exhibit general intelligence rivalling human capabilities across various tasks.

With great power comes great responsibility. The future of AI will not be solely dictated by technological advancements but by the ethical frameworks we establish, the policies we implement and the inclusivity we ensure. It's a journey of co-creation, where businesses, technologists, policymakers and the general public collaborate to shape an AI-driven future that's beneficial for all.

The capabilities of AI will continue to grow and work together, evolving into new systems and models.

Even the best tools and models we have today will improve to unrecognisable levels. As such, the crucial thing to remember when it comes to implementing AI across your business is that it will not stand still, and so being adaptable and evolving along with the technology available will be the best way to extract value from it. With technology evolving at such a rate, it's even more crucial to have the right people with the right skills in your company to interact with and develop your AI tools and projects.

I invite you to approach AI with an open mind. Understand its origins, grasp its current applications and actively participate in its future formulation. Comprehending AI is not about mastering the technical minutiae but about appreciating its potential, its implications and its transformative power. The aim in this chapter is not just to demystify AI but to empower you with the discernment to harness its capabilities judiciously and innovatively.

Key types of AI

While the phrases 'artificial intelligence' and 'machine learning' are often used interchangeably, they are not the same thing. AI is the catch-all term that refers to getting a machine to do something that usually requires human intelligence. ML is a more specific type of AI that enables a machine to learn on its own by analysing data to improve its performance over time, and it is just one of several types of AI at your disposal.

As you explore the ways you could use AI within your company to boost your productivity and growth, it's helpful to understand the different types of AI available and the opportunities they present.

Machine learning

ML enables machines to learn from data by training algorithms to recognise patterns in data and make predictions based on that data. It's used for things like image recognition, fraud detection and segmentation.

This is the AI you want to use if you're looking to automate repetitive tasks. If you've got employees working on things like manual data input, looking for patterns or detecting anomalies in data sets, AI can take on these tasks to free up employees for more strategic tasks.

When it comes to AI implementation, these are your quick wins. According to Microsoft's Global 2023 Work Trend Index Report, workers are most comfortable using AI for analytical work (79%), admin (76%), and creative work (73%).[9]

Deep learning is a subset of ML that involves training neural networks to recognise patterns in complex data. This is useful for tasks that involve large amounts of unstructured data, such as image and speech recognition. You can use deep learning to uncover insights that would take a massive amount of time to identify manually, such as analysing written customer reviews and identifying common themes that can help you improve your product or service. Deep learning can take a series of video clips and find similarities between them or analyse part of an image and complete it.

Computer vision

CV is the branch of AI that enables machines to see, recognise and process images in ways similar to humans. It's a multi-disciplinary field that is a sub-field of computer science, AI and ML. It makes use of general learning algorithms and uses pattern recognition to emulate the ability to see and perceive.

CV relies on Convolutional Neural Networks (CNNs). Computers are first trained on massive amounts of visual data, where they process the imagery and label various objects on them to understand their composition and context. They look for patterns in those objects to understand common characteristics in the visual data until it can correctly identify the overall object.

Images dominate the internet – over three billion images are shared each day. And we now have the computing power needed to analyse this data, CV is a booming field that has grown exponentially over the past few years, achieving huge improvements in the accuracy rates over the past decade, to the point that today's computer vision AI systems are more accurate than humans.

The earliest experiments in computer vision began in the 1950s, but it wasn't put to commercial use till the 1970s, when it was used to differentiate typed text from handwritten text. But today, CV has evolved into a reliable and mature system that generates cost savings and efficiency gains. It has proven accuracy across dozens of sectors, including retail, insurance, agriculture, healthcare, transportation, finance and facilities management. It has a wide variety of uses, such as detecting defects in product lines, early tumour detection, identifying intruders and theft detection, monitoring crops, traffic flow analysis and customer tracking.

Natural Language Processing

NLP is what enables machines to understand and interpret human language. You'll have seen NLP at work in chatbots that can interpret and respond to your queries, or any time you ask Alexa or Siri for help, or even when Grammarly detects the sentiment of what you've written. ChatGPT and other AI writing tools use NLP to understand and respond to your prompts.

If you look around, you'll notice this sort of AI has been a part of your everyday for some time, predicting what you're going to write next in an email, translating social media posts written in a different language, filtering emails into your spam folder.

NLP tools have clear business benefits, but it's likely that there will be a certain amount of anticipation from employees about this type of AI. Some will be wondering if this will put them out of a job, or if their jobs will significantly change as a result of incorporating these tools.

Incorporating NLP into your business strategy will start with helping employees to see that building meaningful partnerships with customers will remain vital for your business. As they come to understand that AI is not a replacement for human connection, and indeed that human intervention is crucial for the successful use of AI across organisations, they will also begin to see their own value within the business.

Robotics

The use of robots to perform tasks that are typically performed by humans is referred to as robotics (or sometimes cobotics). It is particularly useful for tasks that are dangerous, repetitive or require a high degree of precision.

In facilities management, robotics might mean floor scrubbers or vacuuming where there is a large floor plan. In healthcare, there are now precision operation robotics tools making it possible to perform operations that would have previously been too difficult or minute for a human to undertake. Other examples of robotics being put to good use include the development of self-driving vehicles, or delivery bots, which are beginning to have some success in restaurant settings. DPD are expanding their successful 2022 pilot of autonomous delivery robots in the UK after an overwhelmingly positive response from the public.

Robotics offers two key benefits – first it can automate large, time-consuming tasks that require no skill, and second (at the other end of the spectrum), it can take on tasks that require a higher amount of precision, removing the risk of human error. This could be particularly helpful in the manufacturing sector – the production line in car manufacturing, for example, already makes use of robotics in some areas, but could be revolutionised within the next decade.

AI types for your business

It's evident that when we talk about AI and implementing AI into your business we're not talking about one product. Even the three key types explained above barely scratch the surface of the transformative capabilities of the technology available to us and currently in development. While many only really know AI through the lens of ChatGPT at the moment, the reality is that these different types of AI are already prevalent in the world you navigate. As you begin to explore where AI can fit into your business, it's worth having an understanding of these different types to assess where the opportunities are for you.

One of the most exciting things about AI is that it feels like it's limited only by our imaginations. There are so many tools and so many use cases, even at this relatively early stage of AI's development. Part of the challenge will be imagining the potential the technology has for your business. A good place to start with this is looking at real-world case studies.

The power of AI: Real-world case studies

While the potential uses of AI tools and tech may differ from sector to sector, the impact of AI is universal. The ability to streamline productions, automate processes and add capacity can help businesses scale and pivot, keeping up with the pace of change and the demand of the customer.

I'll now explore some of the most common established and emerging uses of AI in businesses that have begun to embrace the technology available to them.

Automation

Arguably the simplest and most cost-effective use of AI, automation offers businesses the ability to release staff from repetitive tasks like data entry, inventory management and even first-line customer support, and redeploy them to higher-value work.

The grocery retailer, Ocado, has become known for its advanced automated warehouses. Their highly efficient Ocado Smart Platform combines AI, robotics and automation to optimise grocery fulfilment.

Their automated warehouses, or Customer Fulfilment Centres, are equipped with a vast array of robots that move along a grid system to retrieve specific grocery items from storage bins. These robots are controlled by AI algorithms that analyse and order data, inventory levels and other factors to determine the most efficient routes and sequences for picking items.

These algorithms learn and improve over time, meaning the optimisation of processes such as inventory management, stock replenishment and order packing keeps getting better and more efficient. This level of automation has enabled Ocado to scale quickly, handling a large volume of orders with high accuracy; it has removed the cost of staffing pickers and packers and has also greatly reduced errors in order fulfilment.

Automation doesn't have to be implemented on such a large scale. Inefficiency is one of the biggest drains on company revenue, and automation AI can be used to reduce the time spent on admin, in meetings and correcting mistakes. These are quick wins for any company implementing AI.

Data entry, as another example, is a fundamental but rudimentary task. It requires precision and attention to detail but it is a repetitive process that automation AI could complete more quickly and accurately, freeing up staff for more complex data work, such as taking meeting minutes, screening CVs, summarising reports and automating project communications.

All of these are easy and cheap to implement and are likely to be met with support from employees, as they are time-draining, low-value tasks. Starting with a full audit of which tasks staff spend the most time on, you can begin to build a map of inefficiencies and tackle low-hanging fruit.

Data analysis

AI brings with it the ability to process and work with huge data sets. It can analyse large volumes of data quickly and extract the insights you need to make business decisions.

In retail, AI is analysing vast amounts of customer data to identify patterns and trends in buying habits. From these insights, we can see correlations between customer demographics and product preferences and browsing habits, and even predict and prevent customer churn. Using AI to mine data for valuable information about what customers want and how they shop can give businesses time and knowledge to serve them better.

In healthcare, Google's DeepMind AI system, Alpha-Fold, has been created to predict the 3D structure of proteins. This highly niche work would be a painstaking task for a human, but with ML a task that would take days has been reduced to minutes. In a recent critical assessment of structure prediction competition, AlphaFold outperformed all other methods in both speed and accuracy. The impact of this work is huge for drug discovery, medical research and understanding diseases at a molecular level, moving research forward quicker than would otherwise have been possible.

Big data analytics is likely to be one of the biggest areas of technology adoption in companies over the next five years, with 75% saying it will be a major area of growth for them.[10] It also ranks top among technologies which are seen as likely to create jobs if they are adopted.

Personalisation

Your customers will now expect a degree of personalisation – if you're still sending communications and don't personalise the basics like name, location and purchase history, then it's safe to say you're considerably behind the curve. Companies are now leveraging their customer data for hyper-personalisation. AI can understand buying habits and trends, and from those generate personalised product recommendations and offers that hit at exactly the right moment.

Amazon, for example, have gone further than this. They now offer personalised search results based on customers' previous searches and browsing history. The entire website journey is personalised, with recommendations, adverts and search results all being generated based on previous search history and previous purchases. This kind of dynamic content generation is possible with AI processing large amounts of customer data.

Customer support

AI chatbots and customer service tools have the potential to save companies hundreds of thousands in salary expenditure. By providing instant responses to customer queries, they improve customer perception in the moments when tensions are at their highest.

As well as handling basic customer support interactions efficiently, AI chatbots have the ability to add value. Make-up brand Sephora is an early AI adopter that's long set its sights on using AI to solve and innovate. Online, their virtual assistant uses AI to help customers find colour-matched cosmetics.

The Sephora app also enhances customer in-store experience with product recommendations and make-up tutorials. Rather than using AI to simply replace customer service representatives dealing with issues, they have employed AI to enhance their offer, adding value and improving the customer experience, with the handy added benefit of cross-selling products.

When looking at AI solutions for customer service, there is value in being able to reduce your headcount, but the real value comes from thinking outside the box about where AI can differentiate you from your competitors and boost customer satisfaction.

AI shouldn't replace human contact altogether, as this is likely to cause more friction in the customer journey. Instead, look at ways AI can reduce friction by answering more rudimentary questions up front, diagnosing problems early or channelling queries to the right teams. Look at ways AI can reduce waiting times or remove the waiting using a callback program.

Product innovation

AI presents so many opportunities to innovate product lines simply through better listening and problem-solving. With ML's ability to search and analyse the marketplace, current trends and consumer preferences, companies can gain detailed insights for product improvements and innovations.

Clothing giant Shein have used this to their advantage, implementing AI to better understand customer preferences and adjusting their product offering accordingly. Their process uses technology to their advantage, maximising value across their supply chain. They start by using AI to find out what styles are trending across search engines and social media. By sifting through huge amounts of data, their technology tells them the styles that are in demand, and also predicts what is likely to be popular in the near future. They're then able to quickly replicate these styles, creating runs large enough to match the demand they've measured, or small enough to test a design's popularity. They reduce spending on marketing because the hype for the products has already occurred, and they've cut wastage by developing products for which there is a demonstrated desire.

Supply chain optimisation

With so many exciting and innovative uses for AI, it's easy to forget that it's through getting the fundamentals right that the biggest cost savings can come. By using AI to make your business foundations secure, you unlock the ability to be more creative elsewhere. Accurate inventory management is one of the quickest wins when it comes to cost-cutting and waste reduction in businesses. ML can predict demand and enhance logistics. With more accurate information and reliable predictions, companies can make better decisions regarding stock levels, transportation, warehousing and overall supply chain planning, leading to cost savings, improved customer service and optimised operations.

Delivery companies like Evri and DHL have managed to outpace Royal Mail using route-optimising AI navigation systems that improve driver efficiency. Their technology can take into account factors including package weight, postage time commitments, traffic patterns through the day and even driver preference for left turns over right. The result is cost-effective package delivery, reductions in fuel consumption, miles driven and delivery time, and, in turn, substantial cost savings and environmental benefits.

Marketing

The huge potential of AI in marketing is a coming-of-age story. In 2018 analysis by McKinsey of over 400 use cases for AI highlighted marketing as the sector where AI could add the greatest value.[11] By 2021 Deloitte had surveyed early AI adopters, and identified that three of the top five AI objectives were for digital marketing uses.[12]

Automating emails has become regular practice within marketing, but AI can now draft those emails as well as automate them, and create the wider content plan that they sit in. This doesn't eliminate the need for marketers, whose creativity in planning eye-catching campaigns that hit home cannot be replaced, and whose technical skills will still be required for set-up, sense-checking and troubleshooting any automated processes, but it does better target their resource.

The real story for AI in marketing is in predictive analytics. AI gives businesses the opportunity to understand their customers better than ever before – not just what they have done and what they are doing, but what they are going to do and what they are likely to want in the future.

This level of insight enables marketing to be fully on the front foot, shifting efforts to being proactive rather than reactive. From creating integrated content strategies for individual niches, to optimising ad copy, to searching through influencer profiles to find the best match for the required audience, AI will undoubtedly save marketers time and make their budget go further.

Generative AI within marketing is growing at a considerable rate. Bloomberg predicts that AI-assisted digital ads are expected to draw US$192 billion annually by 2032.[13] Companies like Treat are using image generators to create product imagery for their ads, and Shopify have added an AI feature to generate optimised product description copy. The recent release of the Barbie movie has shown how AI can be used in marketing to create substantial hype. From the

'Barbiefication' selfie generator to personalised Barbie quizzes, the makers of Barbie have used AI to enable fans to bring themselves into the franchise, giving them a sense of belonging and identification and Barbie a constant stream of user-generated content.

Summary

In this chapter I have given you a broader understanding of AI and considered how its definition has evolved over time. I have analysed what we mean when we talk about AI, delving into the specifics of ML, NLP and robotics, and then looked at how these are being deployed in the real world in cases such as automation, personalisation and product innovation.

THREE
The AI Landscape

In this chapter I want to showcase some of the innovators in the AI space, organisations that have deployed AI across their business to improve customer experience, streamline operational efficiency or improve and diversify their revenue streams. I'll delve into specific use cases across sectors including healthcare, financial services, retail, manufacturing and entertainment. After this I'll set out the global landscape, putting into context the different drivers and blockers for AI usage in different countries around the world.

Surveying the AI ecosystem

Traditional business leaders today face two related challenges. First, the landscape has changed beyond all recognition, and second, it continues to shift at an increasingly rapid rate. Leaders now operate in what is known as a complex system, which is characterised by an evolving environment where a number of different components are constantly interacting with one another.

To illustrate this, when consumers make a retail purchase rather than a decision based on a cost-value judgement, they now may also be taking into account the environmental process of production, the ethical position of the producer and retailer, the celebrities or influencers promoting the product, and the experience of purchasing, whether in store or online. There is a huge set of variables for businesses to consider, and they can be different for each individual and each purchase.

It's hard for businesses to predict what will garner success. What works in one instance may not work a second time or in a different set of circumstances, due to the evolution of these factors. Consequently, instead of relying on extrapolation, the imperative has now shifted to adaptability, learning and innovation.

Organisations are adopting technological solutions like AI to help them become more adaptable to the ever-shifting set of circumstances with which they're grappling. Despite this widespread adoption of technology, overall customer satisfaction seems to be in decline. A study done over thirty years in the Swedish banking industry shows that customer sentiment has gone down despite the banking industry consistently being one of the most prevalent adopters of technology.[14] In Chapter One I discussed the phenomenon known as the expectation overflow – consumers become accustomed to services previously seen as added extras, expect them as standard and view it as a deficit when the service doesn't live up to that expectation. The result of this is that where consumers have seen the rapid evolution of technology, situations where that tech is not used, or not used well, lead to a poor experience. This means that those who stand out in the marketplace are the companies who are innovating at speed, continuously looking at ways to disrupt their industry and improve their customers' experience.

Let's explore some examples of major players and innovations in the AI space, as well as companies successfully using AI to stay ahead of the curve. While generative AI (like ChatGPT or Midjourney) is dominating headlines at the moment, the AI sector is astonishingly large, covering transportation, health, manufacturing and robotics.

Cloud AI companies are some of the largest in the sector, offering technology covering the entire life cycle of AI, hosted and delivered through cloud computing platforms. These include Google, Microsoft, IBM, Amazon Web Services and Alibaba Cloud. Alibaba is the largest technology and e-commerce company in China and its cloud computing arm has grown to be one of the world's leading providers. It is capable of complex image recognition, video content analysis, NLP, text analysis, speech recognition and translation services. Alibaba has been involved in smart city initiatives across China, using AI to improve urban planning, traffic management, public services and more.

In transportation there are companies making strides towards autonomous vehicles, developing delivery drones and improving vehicular safety. Pony.ai have raised US$400 million from Toyota and have already developed a self-driving ride-sharing fleet in Guangzhou, China. Nauto is an AI-powered learning platform for driver behaviour. It uses cameras and sensors to monitor the road and driver behaviour in real time, detect potential hazards, reduce distracted driving and prevent risky behaviours and collisions.

AI in e-commerce is perhaps the most visible form we see across industry. In marketing, sales, product development and customer experience, AI providers are helping retailers to use the massive amounts of data they already collect to optimise demand planning, increase revenue and improve targeting. Icertis (who have gained several large clients, including Microsoft) uses large language models (LLMs) to take insights from contracts and turn them into actionable data and competitive advantage, in turn helping companies to realise the full value of their commercial agreements.

Sector-specific implications of AI

The embeddedness of AI across sectors is uneven, but, as the speed of development further increases, AI will offer more in every sector. However, much as it took more than forty years from the invention of electricity to widespread consumer usage, sector take-up will depend on the potential of the technology to transform the company's ability to produce at speed and more conveniently.

Healthcare

AI is making inroads across the healthcare sector, specifically around diagnostics and treatment. AI algorithms are being used to analyse medical images to aid early detection of diseases and make more accurate diagnoses. For instance, AI-enabled mammography systems have shown a 30% reduction in false negatives.[15]

Tempus is an AI company specialising in 'data-driven precision medicine'. They use patient data to deliver personalised and optimised treatments. On the other side of the coin, Suki was created to support clinicians in note-taking and adapts to the individual with repeated use, meaning it becomes more efficient over time. Freenome is making waves in the healthcare sector, spotting signs of cancer earlier than ever through screenings and diagnostic tests to identify disease-associated patterns in blood tests, enabling early intervention. AI algorithms have achieved 92% accuracy in predicting heart failure within one year.[16]

These are costly applications of AI, but there are also grassroots opportunities to capitalise on the innovative potential of AI within the healthcare sector. In the UK some NHS trusts have begun to use AI automation and data analysis to improve projects. These initiatives gather ideas and feedback from frontline healthcare professionals, group and sort them, and then action those that can increase efficiency, save money or improve patient outcomes. For example, in one NHS trust the data collected identified time was being wasted and patient safety was being compromised in emergency situations when staff weren't able to source the drugs and equipment needed quickly enough. As a result of these insights, the trust implemented emergency grab bags with tamper-proof security tags, identifying when a grab bag was complete with all the necessary stock or if it needed to be refilled. On just one ward, this led to twenty-two hours a week of time saved, totalling a financial saving of £19,000 a year.[17]

Financial services

Nowhere has AI had such a disruptive effect as the financial services industry. Everything from the way banks serve their customers to the way financial fraud is detected has been transformed by AI. The rise of app-based banking has left traditional operators scrambling to catch up, seemingly signalling the end of the high street bank.

The amount of data that financial service institutions have at their disposal puts them at a significant advantage, so it's not surprising that it has been finance and finance security organisations that have driven forward the use of AI both in their operations and in creating more customer-centric services. The swathes of personal data include transaction histories, location data risk profiles, credit ratings, product usage, brand loyalty and even online search history and campaign engagement.

Alongside that, they have had to battle the significant disadvantages that come with being an established sector – for example, legacy technology, disconnected and scattered data, silos and lack of communication or collaboration. These disadvantages have made it hard to create a cohesive customer view and, in turn, leverage AI in banking solutions. It's unsurprising that it has been new players in the finance sector who have disrupted the market, leaving traditional establishments to catch up.

Over the past five years, those traditional institutions have made efforts to close the gap. AI solutions have almost entirely replaced human-based customer service in consumer banking, with chatbots predicted to save banks more than US$11 billion in 2023.[18] Fraud detection has also been revolutionised. AI algorithms can analyse vast amounts of financial data to identify patterns and anomalies, meaning a reduction in fraud losses. AI-powered fraud detection systems have reduced false positives by 40%.[19]

Retail

The retail sector is arguably putting AI to use in some of the most fun and interesting ways – I've already mentioned Sephora's colour-matching service, but this isn't the only way AI is pushing the boundaries in improving customer experience.

ASOS have begun using an AI-powered virtual assistant called Enki, which asks customers a series of questions and then gives them personalised style advice. Retailers that implemented such systems have seen a 15–20% uplift in their conversion rates.[20]

In supermarkets, AI is used to optimise store layout, tracking things like customer journeys through the shop, eye movements across shelves, and patterns in the kinds of products being bought at particular times in the week and throughout the day. This is helping retailers to better predict and optimise their inventory levels, reducing the risk of stock shortages and surpluses. Some are also using AI to improve in-store experience, like lighting and temperature adjustments to make the store more comfortable for shoppers.

H&M is one of the world's largest fashion retailers, with 5,000 stores across seventy-four countries. Over the space of three years, H&M built a robust AI and analytics function, becoming an industry leader in AI. Their chief data and analytics officer attributes their success to their implementation of five key conditions:

1. **Culture of courage:** Dare to do new things, dare to fail. Failing is a learning opportunity.

2. **Compass over map:** Try not to plan too long. Trust the needle of the compass and look at the direction you're moving in rather than the destination. If something fails, pivot.

3. **Deploy or die:** Test things in reality. Create a minimum viable product, test it and iterate.

4. **Create conditions:** Measurement is crucial, but instead of measuring downward in specific silos, measure across the business. Measure customer impact, measure the output of new algorithms, ask new questions often.

5. **Amplified intelligence:** The goal of using AI at H&M is not to replace people, it's to amplify existing talent and processes. Those looking to implement AI for the sole reason of reducing headcount are unlikely to see the long-term value or impact of their AI projects.

Using these five conditions, H&M have successfully innovated the customer experience, not just online but also in their bricks-and-mortar stores, where AI technology is giving them the competitive edge.

They have introduced RFID technology so they can track inventory in real time. While this means they can optimise stock levels, it also enables them to go a step further: they use receipts and returns to evaluate products that are in demand and those that aren't selling well so they can adjust stock and promotions by location. It also gives them the insight to predict what the market wants and when – maximising their profits by ensuring they have the right amount of stock – and reduce the need for discounts. RFID technology also enables the fashion giant to extend its online personalised recommendation experience to physical stores. Online customers can see exactly which items and sizes are available in a specific store, and in-store customers can scan labels to see if the item is available online or in other locations.

H&M's automated warehouses make picking, packing and shipping items more efficient. Ultimately, this allows the company to offer next-day deliveries for most European markets.

Manufacturing

Across the manufacturing industry, AI is streamlining processes, enhancing efficiency and improving quality control. It is empowering companies to simplify operations and minimise costs through the integration of AI technologies to give them data-driven insights, predictive analytics and intelligent automation to achieve efficiency. They use this data analysis to better understand where wastage is coming from and create processes that eliminate unnecessary steps or errors.

Manufacturers are also using AI for predictive maintenance, both in their equipment and in their production lines. By analysing sensor data, AI algorithms can anticipate equipment failures before they occur, enabling companies to perform maintenance proactively, reducing downtime and avoiding costly breakdowns. On average, companies that have begun to employ AI in this way have increased productivity by 25%, reduced breakdowns by 70% and lowered maintenance costs by 25%.[21]

Quality control has also become easier and more reliable by using AI to eliminate human error. For example, AI-enabled computer-vision systems detect defects in manufactured products in real time by gathering 3D information on the product's surfaces, which could lead to reduced defect rates by up to 90%.[22] Real-time AI photo analysis goes even further than that – not just identifying defects, but classifying them and putting them into context with wider information about errors and defects that enable manufacturers to identify patterns and make changes to improve their processes.

AI can also enable smart inventory management. By leveraging historical data and demand patterns, manufacturers can accurately forecast demand, optimise inventory levels and minimise storage costs while ensuring timely deliveries. Additionally, AI-driven supply chain optimisation ensures the efficient movement of raw materials, reducing lead times and operational expenses.

Finally, AI-driven robotics and automation have revolutionised production lines, enhancing precision and speed while reducing labour costs. Collaborative robots, or cobots, work safely alongside human operators, boosting productivity and freeing employees from repetitive tasks.

With such a wide array of uses in the manufacturing sector, AI tools are already empowering businesses to make data-driven decisions, enhance efficiency and reduce expenses, ultimately leading to increased profits and a competitive edge in the market. As AI continues to evolve, its potential to transform manufacturing processes and yield greater financial benefits will only grow for those who are willing to look for and embrace the opportunities.

Entertainment and leisure

The entertainment and leisure industry is another area where AI is slowly beginning to show the transformative impact it can have. ML is enabling more personalised content and increasing engagement in a post-Covid environment. The sector was hit hard by the pandemic and is arguably the one that requires the most help to recover. For starters, predictive analytics make it easier to predict and staff for demand trends and explore alternative revenue for downtimes, which is helping venues bridge the gap while leisure attendance recovers.

Virtual reality and AI-powered gaming are creating immersive crossover experiences, propelling the industry towards new frontiers and re-engaging customers with new experiences.

THE AI LANDSCAPE

AI in hospitality is reducing waste by understanding occupancy numbers and increasing operational efficiency with dynamic pricing based on demand and occupancy levels. Surge pricing has already become commonplace in holiday pricing and, more recently, in taxi pricing. It's likely that this will become a more widely used practice across the entertainment industry with 'peak' and 'off-peak' prices becoming more precise and localised.

Guest experience is improving through virtual tours before booking and then via integrating AI into lighting, temperature control and entertainment systems, making stays more pleasant and more energy-efficient.

Odeon Cinemas are using AI to gain a competitive edge in a fast-evolving industry. With competitor cinemas taking a boutique, 'experience-driven' approach, Odeon have had to 'work smarter' to keep up. They have automated ticketing and customer service to reduce manual work and provide a faster service. In their marketing, AI provides personalised film recommendations to increase ticket sales. Using AI algorithms, Odeon analyse customer data such as viewing history and ratings to tailor suggestions, enhancing customer satisfaction and loyalty. They're also using predictive analytics to forecast demand for screenings. This has enabled them to optimise film scheduling, reducing underoccupied screenings and opening up new revenue streams, such as using empty screens for Kids Club screenings.

Global trends in approaching AI

Across the globe, AI is being used, developed and accepted in diverse ways. The US, China, Germany and Japan have all made significant investment and substantial strides in AI development and implementation, and all approach the use of AI in different ways. Both public opinion and policy shape the adoption and regulation of AI in each country. Some are embracing it as the new standard for business and governance, while others are more cautious, concerned about where AI could lead without proper regulation and safeguards in place.

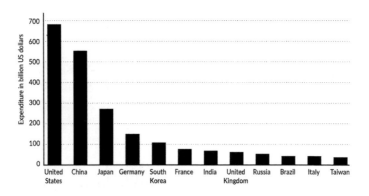

Leading countries by gross research and development expenditure worldwide in 2022 (in billion US dollars)

Note: Worldwide, 2021; derived from purchasing power parity calculations. Source: IRI; ID 732247

The US and North America

AI innovation has surged forward in the US and North America, with significant investment made in both public and private sectors. The government has allocated substantial funding to AI research and development initiatives through agencies like the National Science Foundation and The Defense Advanced Research Projects Agency. Leading technology companies such as Google, Microsoft and IBM are actively investing in AI research, development and applications.

A 2021 study found that 45% of Americans were equally concerned and excited about the possibilities of AI, with many more expecting to lose their job to AI and needing to retrain to find a new one within the next decade.[23] A study by Boston Consulting Group in 2023 found that frontline workers tend not to use AI to increase productivity and that managers/directors are currently the main users.[24]

As communication around use cases improves, the US has huge potential for AI development due to their appetite for investment and a willingness from senior leaders to experiment and implement. Before this can happen, though, work needs to be done to allay the fears of the working population. Centralised state education programmes helping people to understand the benefits of AI and the positive impact on capacity and job creation could smooth the implementation and adoption journey for businesses.

China

China has rapidly emerged as a global AI powerhouse driven by large investments from both the public and private sectors. The Chinese government has set ambitious goals to become a world leader in AI by 2030. Initiatives like the New Generation AI Development Plan and the Next Generation AI Major Project aim to advance AI research, promote innovation and develop a robust AI ecosystem. Chinese tech giants, including Alibaba, Baidu and Tencent, are heavily investing in AI technologies and applications.

Whereas AI for surveillance is one of the most pervasive fear factors in the US, in China it has one of the strongest markets. Social-scoring algorithms are being developed to measure people's amenability to social structures and government policy. Social scoring tracks millions of data points for travelling, buying, education, work and socialising habits to gauge how social a person is; it then ranks them and gives certain opportunities to that individual. China also uses AI to police, with facial recognition databases slightly more advanced than those used in the UK and the EU. As the amount of data collected grows, the ability to track and police using AI becomes more and more sophisticated.

A 2022 report by Reuters discovered that China had conducted nine tenders on software that could be used with facial recognition to identify a person as Uyghur, then connecting with police warning systems.[25] With such advanced AI usage in government, businesses have the advantage of widespread acceptance of AI, making implementation much easier. China has the data and the investment to surge ahead and is likely to become a comprehensive use case for an AI-assisted society. It has already been coined as the first 'AI-tocracy', exporting huge amounts of AI technology, dwarfing its contributions in other frontier technology sectors, and posing serious problems for regulators and policy makers across the world who don't have the control or innovation levels that China does.

Japan

Japan has long been at the forefront of technological innovation, and it's no surprise that their approach to AI has been proactive – they invest in research and development to implement AI in practical ways across healthcare, mobility and robotics. They have cultivated public–private partnerships (for example, the AI Bridging Cloud Infrastructure), which look to accelerate research and promote collaboration by drawing together experts and researchers from academia, industry and government. Japanese enterprises including Toyota, Sony and SoftBank have already invested heavily in AI applications. In 2021 Toyota invested £200 million in thirty-six AI start-ups, exploring applications ranging from video analytics to self-driving cars.

AI is more socially accepted in Japan than it currently is in the West. Innovation is viewed as a way to ensure businesses are productive with a smaller workforce, and AI is seen as a means of support to a shrinking labour force. A study conducted in 2021 reported that the Japanese workforce don't have the same concerns over job loss, as there is a social expectation that workers will be retrained via government and enterprise initiatives.[26] The study concluded that in countries where there was a lower rate of job security, there was greater fear and less acceptance of AI.

Germany

Having established the 'AI made in Germany' initiative, Germany have squarely planted their flag in the ground. The German government are pouring funds into supporting AI research and innovation, and with such a strong manufacturing base in the country, AI technologies have quickly been integrated into industrial automation and robotics.

AI risk management across the EU is characterised by a more comprehensive range of legislation, tailored to specific digital environments. This means there are (or are planned to be) requirements placed on high-risk AI in socio-economic processes such as education, welfare, politics and security, as well as government use of AI and regulated consumer products. Countries within the EU will be required to have a higher

THE AI LANDSCAPE

level of public transparency, and therefore increased influence, over the design of AI systems.

This means that while Germany have a high level of investment in AI, they are also bought into controlled regulation around both development and use. This may mean higher costs and will certainly mean higher restrictions associated with developing AI systems.

UK

With AI having been recognised as a priority area for economic growth in the UK, and an investment of £1 billion dedicated to its development, the relatively slow start in AI development and adoption in the UK is set to accelerate. The Alan Turing Institute and the British AI Strategy aim to position the UK as global leaders in AI research and applications.

The UK is hindered, however, by the confusion created by Brexit and what exiting the EU means for GDPR and data protection laws. This has slowed down, and in some cases completely stopped, the data collection and sharing that have enabled the speed of innovation and development seen elsewhere in the world. Where AI development has been successful in the UK, it is led by business and enterprise, where there have been large investments made in areas such as manufacturing, cybersecurity and supply chain.

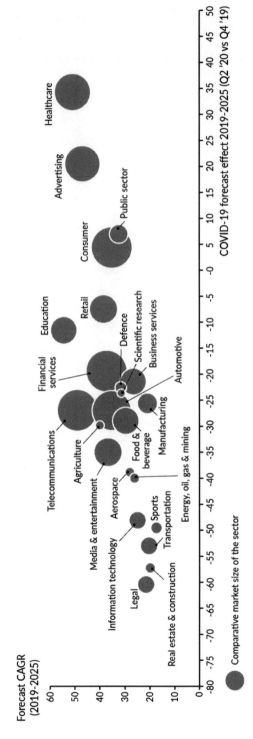

Global AI software revenue by industry: Covid-19 impact vs 2019–2025 compound annual growth rate.

Sources: Tractica; Omida

Summary

In Chapter Three I have discussed the major players in the AI landscape, the speed at which these companies are developing AI solutions, and the ways in which these are impacting particular sectors, including financial services, retail and manufacturing. After looking at sectoral implications, I then moved on to think about the global trends and the ways in which different countries are interacting with and regulating AI.

FOUR
Preparing Your Organisation For AI

Over the next few chapters of the book, I'm going to turn to more practical thinking to guide you through the process of creating your own roadmap for AI implementation. I've explored the theory of and laid the foundations for the ways in which AI is being successfully used in businesses. In this chapter I'll look at how you can assess your business readiness for AI. I'll explain the four core principles of AI, and then I'll outline the issues you need to consider for an integrated AI strategy. A huge part of ensuring AI success is having the right people in place and the right skills available to you, which means attracting the best talent on the market. Finally, I'll give a short overview of ethics in AI. It's worth pointing out that, as a topic, the ethics of AI deserves a book of its own, but as this is not the main consideration of this guidebook, and knowing I cannot hope to do it justice in the space I have here, I'll only briefly touch on this.

Identifying AI opportunities

Digital transformation can be costly. It takes time, resources and budget. In 2022 global spending on digital change projects reached US$1.8 trillion.[27] Despite this, studies from 2020 to 2022 show that almost 70% of these projects fail.[28]

The question 'Why?' has been asked dozens of times, and each time it has been answered with a dozen explanations. McKinsey's study shows that up to 70% of these failed projects did not reach their potential due to employee resistance.[29] Another study shows that digital change projects are 1.6 times more likely to succeed with a dedicated chief digital officer overseeing them.[30] In another, 75% of executives state that their business functions compete instead of collaborating on their digital projects.[31]

Employee resistance, lack of leadership and interdepartmental rivalry are all symptoms of a broader, cultural issue – a lack of readiness for change. Jumping into a large digital project before the company is prepared to handle or accept that change is likely to end in failure.

With AI, this is exacerbated by the speed of development and the sheer number of tools and use cases. It's a mammoth task to wade through the options and evaluate where to identify cost reduction, value creation and/or operational efficiency. Understanding where to replace human effort, where to blend human and digital capabilities, and where the human answer is still the best is key to creating a future-proof business. That's why assessing your readiness in key areas, and then creating a roadmap for change with additional support in the areas that need it, will increase your chances of success.

What are businesses looking for?

The gap between winners and losers is widening each day. Traditional sectors are in upheaval, no longer offering stable returns, but rapid growth in the current economic circumstances, with businesses facing so many uncertainties, seems incredibly difficult. Leaders are, of course, looking for an edge or a way to join the 6% of companies that set the pace for AI competition, but billions of dollars are wasted on tech investments every year in search of a silver bullet, without the proper foundations being put in place to make those changes successful.[32] Change has never been more urgent, and yet a 70% failure rate says something important about how these projects are being implemented.[33]

CEOs face some tough questions about adapting in a changing world and building for the future. Businesses need a blueprint that accelerates their change agendas – a proven guide for growth and innovation – but many don't know where to start. Many more have begun and stagnated after not reaping the initial benefits.

Core AI principles

Across the organisations I've worked with, I've seen repeatedly that the culture of an organisation can either facilitate or hinder the implementation of digital initiatives. Once you've identified the opportunities for AI in your business, the next step is to assess your readiness for change. New projects often elicit a sense of fear from the workforce, and the overall culture into which change is introduced will impact how that fear is expressed and handled.

I'll look now at the most common characteristics of organisations that have benefitted from successful outcomes with their AI transformation projects.

Agility

Around 86% of software development companies are agile, and with good reason.[34] Adopting an agile mindset and methodologies could give you an edge on your competitors, with companies adopting agile seeing an average 60% growth in revenue and profit as a result. Our research has shown that agile companies are 43% more likely to succeed in their digital projects.

Why does agile working make such a difference? It might be the ability to fail fast. The agile mindset enables teams to push through setbacks and see failures as opportunities to learn rather than reasons to stop. Agile teams have a resilience that is critical to success when trying to build and implement AI solutions to problems.

Leaders who display this kind of perseverance are 4 times more likely to deliver their intended outcomes. Developing the determination to regroup and push ahead within their leadership team is considerably easier if they are perceived as authentic in their commitment to embedding AI into the company. Leaders can begin to eliminate roadblocks by listening to their teams and supporting them when issues or fears arise. That means proactively adapting when changes occur – whether this involves more delegation, bringing in external support or reprioritising resources.

Using this approach should lead to behavioural change across the organisation. This should start with commitment from the top to new ways of working, and an investment in skills, processes and dedicated positions to scale agile behaviours. From here, agile principles should be embedded into teams, who then need to become used to working cross-functionally through sprints, rapid escalation and a fail-fast-and-learn approach.

To help this, I suggest you follow these five steps:

1. **Start with why:** Agile is a means to an end, not the goal. Clearly communicate the goal you're working towards. Demonstrate the value of agile and guard against backsliding into old ways of working. The goal is not agile itself. The goal should be a clear outcome that agile working can better help you to reach.

2. **Adopt the principles and adapt the practices:** Agile is an adaptable methodology. Understand, adapt and actively promote agile principles and ways of working, but don't use them as a rod. These principles should be adapted to each team and their needs.[35]

3. **Align to empower:** Give people the ability to act autonomously to help them take ownership of their work and act creatively in their role. It's this autonomy that ensures agile teams can move as fast as they do. If team members are well aligned and working towards the same goals and timescales, it's easier to give them autonomy within those boundaries.

4. **Learn and adapt at speed:** Agile puts a premium on feedback and learning. Willingness to adapt is more important than following a plan. This needs to be the case across the whole

organisation, top to bottom, meaning leaders need to be enthusiastically willing to adapt to the needs of the business, new technologies and new ways of working.

5. **Consider and contain the key risks:** Giving people autonomy within boundaries and allowing them to fail without fear of blame can yield significant benefits, but you need to ensure that if they fail, your organisation can cope with the fallout. If you identify a single-point-of-failure risk within your organisation, be ready to increase the support as required.

Trust

One of the things we've discovered to be almost universally true is that AI transformation comes with a considerable amount of fear from the wider workforce. This fear can act as a barrier to wider adoption of AI technology and so it's important to address colleagues' concerns early in the process.

To help people adjust to the potential shift, I suggest the following three things:

1. **Honesty:** There are several ways you can help to ease worries across your organisation, but first and foremost it's crucial to be honest. If AI will lead to job losses and redeployments, be upfront about it. Building trust begins with honesty and integrity. Giving people a sense of certainty as

early as possible, whether that's reassuring them that they will be retained or putting in place support for redeployment, will help reduce AI anxiety.

2. **Be creative about how to support people:** Look at the skills you require across your business and create an environment of continuous learning, focusing on adapting skills and roles to the future shape of the business. Empower employees to gain skills in data science, data analytics, ML and project management. Consider job shares, part-time hours or flexible contracts where redeployment isn't appropriate.

3. **Explore applications:** Encourage team members to find ways that AI will support them to be more efficient and increase their value. Help them to see AI as another tool they can work with rather than as a replacement for their capabilities, and enable them to gain the knowledge, skills and experience to stay current and thrive in the workplace of the future.

Customer orientation

Those organisations that centre their AI projects around customer ease and experience tend to see more successful outcomes. Ask yourself these three questions and try out some of the things I suggest in my answers before starting:

1. **How can I improve the customer journey?**

   Consider doing a 'mystery shop' of your own process to understand where friction occurs. When you have an idea of areas that could be improved, look at the ways AI could be applied to remove barriers or inconveniences. Zara's trial of self-checkouts in their stores was originally met with resistance, but when customers began to benefit from shorter waiting times, they soon accepted the change as a success.

2. **How can I save my customers time and/or money?**

   Electrical giant, Phillips, cleverly responded to customer concerns about energy costs, despite not being an energy company. By pivoting towards smart home technology and energy-efficient solutions for their customers, they found a way to use AI to support their customers in saving time and money (remotely starting the washing machine, smart thermostats, occupancy sensors) while encouraging them to buy Phillips products.

3. **How can I better align my product/service to customer need?**

   Try surveying your customers to find out what they're looking for from your product or service. It's easy to assume you know exactly what their pain points are, but as customer expectations shift so rapidly in today's digital world, so too does customer need. Monzo asked their customers what support they'd like from their bank, and the overwhelming response was help with increasing savings. In response, Monzo implemented AI to analyse customers' transaction data and automatically categorise expenses, offering spending summaries, savings targets and real-time notifications to help customers track their expenses, identify areas of overspending and encourage better saving habits.

Innovation

Finally, it's companies that encourage and reward innovative thinking at every level of their organisation that see the most success with their AI and digital projects. Embedding innovation into an organisation often requires a change in mindset – one where experimentation is rewarded and failed projects are seen as an important part of the learning process. To create an environment that fosters innovation, it's important that people are permitted to fail and empowered to take calculated risks.

Consider the following aspects of your business to understand if it is a place where innovation can thrive:

- Are there any incentives in place to encourage innovative thinking and problem-solving?
- Do employees feel empowered to make decisions or feed back ideas to their managers?

- Are team members disincentivised from taking risks due to fear of repercussions or attitudes?

- Is there a team or forum in place to research and support innovation across the business?

- Are leaders open to hearing ideas and feedback from their team members? Do they introduce new ideas and/or support ideas when they're presented? Are they, themselves, open to change?

Setting the groundwork for innovation, along with addressing the other core principles, will create a stable foundation for AI implementation in a way that is helpful, strategic and lasting.

Strategy

Once you've considered the four core principles and you feel your organisation has the foundation in place to successfully adopt AI, you can begin planning your AI projects. One of the key factors for digital transformation success is strategy. Boston Consulting Group have done extensive research into digital transformation success and discovered that among their clients a clear, well-communicated, integrated strategy can flip chances of long-term success from 30% to almost 80%.[36]

In my own work, I have discovered that while most companies will have a dedicated strategy planning phase before they begin their AI projects, only about 20% put in place an integrated strategy with clear goals that relate back to their business objectives. The ones that do push forward integration are more likely to see return on their investment. Bringing AI into a business will be considerably more successful if the application of the technology is well thought-out and scaled across the company.

What is an integrated strategy?

An integrated strategy is one that looks at all the areas of the business and considers all the processes that might enhance competitiveness, efficiency, effectiveness or market share.

I suggest taking the following six actions to make sure you have an integrated strategy for introducing AI into your business:

1. **Define the overarching vision:** Bring your leaders together to set a clear aspiration for implementing AI that links to your competitive advantage and value creation.

2. **Embed AI into the overall business strategy:** AI shouldn't be an add-on; instead, make sure that your business goals require the success of AI implementation.

3. **Anchor around business use cases:** Focus on just a few prioritised business cases with clear

outcomes and committed, accountable personnel who champion AI. The success of these will help you build momentum and increase support across the business.

4. **Ensure a clear tech and data strategy:** Scope out the AI requirements based on both your business and staff needs. This means understanding the problems and getting advice on the tech to solve them so that any solutions don't end up creating more problems. There will be multiple AI solutions to many of these problems, so make sure there is a clear process for gathering information and advice for decision-making.

5. **Align your leaders and create a change agenda:** Make sure everyone is on the same page on what it will take to drive the change required in skills and behaviours across the organisation. Embed these actions into your leadership team's targets.

6. **Develop a roadmap with prioritised initiatives:** A good roadmap should use dynamic governance processes to provide transparency around prioritised activities, deliverables, timelines and financial and human resources.

The starting point must be a clear vision. Be bold in setting your aspiration for AI. Shoot high and ensure you have the resources you need to reach your goals – for example, a multi-year funding plan. Finally, embed data in your digital and business strategy. Know what you're going to collect and what to use it for.

Cultivating AI skills within your organisation

As I discussed in the first chapter, people are the number one factor contributing to the success of digital transformation projects. In my experience, companies who can identify, attract and retain the best talent are almost 50% more likely to succeed in their transformation efforts.

The organisations that see meaningful success are those that employ top people and give them central, career-advancing roles. They also ensure they have a diverse team with a good mix of digital expertise and general organisational experience.

War for talent

Our relationship with work has changed. As technology has moved forward, we have become better connected and the world has become more accessible. All this means more choice for employees as well as consumers. Standing out against a global backdrop and offering flexible, remote, exciting work opportunities will require creative ways to attract and retain talent.

When talking about AI implementation, it's easy to get wrapped up in the tactics, the technology and the techniques involved in bringing about change, but this needs to be framed within the context of those delivering the change. The teams enacting and adopting the change are the crucial piece of the puzzle when looking at successful transformation. Although job losses are a primary concern when considering AI, having the right talent in place is the key to success. Focusing on getting the skills you need within the business early on is a critical factor, not least because the competition for talent is extremely high, particularly in digital engineering and ML.

For companies looking to embrace digital technology, that talent will need to bridge the skills gap that reflects a significant shift in the value chain. Society is rapidly moving away from the industrial age when products are manufactured and sold to consumers, towards a model where data and knowledge are harnessed through specialist expertise to deliver quality services to users. This requires a different level and type of skill and creativity than has been in demand in recent decades. The businesses who secure the talent capable of this level of creativity alongside displaying the technical implementation skills to bring it to fruition will gain the edge over their competitors.

In a post-Covid world, employees have a better understanding of and greater appreciations for their work–life balance. People have enjoyed the flexibility of working from home and the freedom of not having to commute every day. After the pandemic ended and businesses began to return to 'business as usual', a huge proportion of workers decided that going back to the office full-time wasn't for them.

In 2022 we experienced the Great Resignation. People left their jobs in droves. After decades of believing that job security was critical, major global events – including a pandemic, economic instability, supply chains breaking down, rapid inflation and strains on basic resources such as water, food and energy – have had a huge impact on people's views on job and income security.

The most rigid companies found themselves losing their best talent to companies willing to be more flexible with their return-to-work policies. As a result, hybrid working patterns have become almost expected as standard practice, and people's motivations and priorities for their work have undergone the biggest shift since the Second World War.

Environmental, social and political issues that have, in the past, had little to do with brands and their external personas have become crucial to the decision-making process of consumers and employees alike. Consumers who are motivated by these values have voted with their wallets, choosing to support the companies that prioritise social good, and employees have voted with their feet, heading to companies that show their commitment to diversity, sustainability, the environment and wellbeing.

Employee value proposition

Word-of-mouth marketing has a far greater power due to the scope of digital channels to disseminate messaging more quickly and widely. This means messaging that has not been created directly by a company, but rather by its customers and employees, will have a wider impact because mobile technology and connectivity has made it possible for anyone to voice their opinion, from anywhere, and be heard almost instantly.

Escaping this reality is increasingly challenging because of the abundance of information shared on social media and review sites. Companies are no longer able to control their own narrative because their stakeholders – customers and employees – communicate directly with other customers and employees to vent their frustrations. The narratives are co-created.

This is where EVP and employer brand come into play. Creating strong messaging around company values, growth opportunities, benefits and wellbeing helps to entice prospective candidates, showing them they'll be part of something that's more than just a job but is, instead, a gateway to learning, growth, development and a greater purpose. Conveying this purpose to top talent is just as important as putting in place annual bonuses and pension plans. People want purpose and they want to buy into companies that can authentically communicate what they stand for and demonstrate the value they create.

Gig economy

The war for talent has led to a change in the way people approach their employment opportunities. With so many organisations running fully remote teams, and platform companies creating global opportunities, the gig economy has boomed. Companies can draw from a diverse talent pool, anywhere in the world, to get work done fast, disrupting the structures that have underpinned the traditional forms of employment and job security.

Many workers, especially those who have embraced the gig economy, appreciate the flexibility that comes with it, and that level of flexibility has become a key factor in attracting and retaining talent.[37] In fact, 54% of the working population is now working flexibly in some form.[38] This has changed how organisations approach recruitment: they have moved away from human resource departments managing employees and towards talent strategy teams that explore how to meet human resources needs.

Twenty-first century skills

Those candidates with the right digital and technical skills have the luxury of taking their pick of the roles. However, while technical skills are easy to screen for, soft skills are much harder to gauge at interview. They're contextual to each organisation, as the soft skills needed are often dependent on the culture and needs of the existing team. It's these soft skills that pose the most significant challenges when implementing change projects. Alongside overcoming the existing corporate culture, changing the prevailing mindsets and attitudes within a business is the core challenge for change projects. Having a strategy to develop these soft skills across teams will give any company a competitive advantage that others will struggle to imitate.

In addition to developing soft skills in individuals, there is a wider challenge for teams to break down silos, collaborate more effectively and work in ways that complement and emphasise individual skills. This challenge needs to be addressed with a practical management framework that can deliver the outcomes but is simple enough to be adopted quickly and without masses of expertise. It needs to be structured enough to deliver results without stifling innovation and autonomy, and it needs to balance business priorities with required timelines and realistic talent development goals.

Attracting and retaining the right talent is important, and directing it towards meaningful outcomes is critical. There are five actions I suggest for cultivating digital leaders across your company:

1. **Show your commitment through your resourcing decisions:** When you begin your digital and AI projects, communicate across the business that the best performers will be involved in them and that they will be career-advancing projects. Reward those individuals who go above and beyond to increase their digital skill set or take the initiative to get to grips with AI that supports their work or their team. Don't be afraid to bring in external experts to fill or support pivotal roles, especially where the requisite digital skills might be in short supply.

2. **Take an open-source approach to finding talent:** Start with a detailed assessment of the skills required, highlighting where the gaps are. Then create a talent acquisition plan that fills these gaps through redeployment, hiring new talent or accessing external resources such as agencies or freelancers.

3. **Ensure effective team composition:** The team needs to be made up of digitally literate people from a wide cross section of business departments to drive new thinking and become champions in their critical areas.

4. **Manage talent dynamically to sustain employee engagement and morale:** Before starting, you need to have processes in place to evaluate and develop team members, rewarding those who do well and replacing

poor performers. It's important to have visible ways to celebrate success and manage morale, especially when things get tough.

5. **Create a talent pipeline:** Critical digital capabilities are in low supply and high demand, so it's important to keep an eye on what talent is needed and when and maintain an open pipeline to fill gaps early. Part of this involves upskilling across the breadth of the company. Digital skills are not just for teams directly involved in digital transformation – they need to be cascaded throughout.

Navigating moral, legal and societal challenges

As AI advances and takes a greater role in society, we must consider the ethical conundrums we'll be facing and the associated risks. We've already seen an instance of a judge using AI in sentencing a case, which has thrown up dozens of questions about human vs AI bias. These cases and their issues will only become more pronounced as AI's abilities grow.

The ethical implications have been thrown into even sharper contrast as AI creators and tech experts call for AI development to slow down while we consider the societal impact the technology could have. A study by Pew Research Center found that 72% of

Americans express concern about AI's potential to impact privacy, while 67% worry about its potential to automate jobs.[39]

Alongside worries around privacy and job losses, concerns are growing around what it means to delegate key decision-making to AI, removing human empathy from situations where it can potentially make all the difference. There is a growing emphasis on fairness, transparency and accountability in AI systems and a heightened focus on the ethical dimensions of AI as society grapples with the complex implications of this rapidly advancing technology.

Data collection and governance

Data security and privacy concerns are among the most pressing issues currently being discussed, and the number of reported data breaches and cyberattacks is increasing. A 2022 government study showed that almost 40% of UK organisations experienced at least one cybersecurity breach in that year, resulting in significant financial losses and reputational damage.[40]

Proportion of UK businesses identifying cyberattacks each year

2017	2018	2019	2020	2021	2022
46%	43%	32%	46%	39%	39%

The rise of deepfake technology, which uses AI to manipulate or fabricate audio and video content, has raised concerns about the potential for misinformation, fraud and privacy invasions. There have already been concerns raised around the impact that AI algorithms and AI-curated information has had on elections. The increase in the use of bots to promulgate information, control narratives and influence public opinion has led to growing cynicism around democratic processes. As a result, there is an increasing demand for robust security measures and ethical guidelines to address these challenges and ensure the responsible deployment of AI systems.

When you begin to explore using AI in your company, you'll need to consider how to collect and use data responsibly. I'll look at this in more detail in Chapter Six, and I'll try to outline some practical ways of doing this.

AI bias

Another area of concern is the presence of biases in AI systems that can impact job opportunities and employment prospects. Studies have shown that AI algorithms used in hiring processes can exhibit biases against certain groups, such as women and minority candidates.

For example, a 2019 study found that an AI recruiting tool developed by a major tech company favoured male candidates over female candidates.[41] Another study in the same year discovered that facial recognition algorithms had higher error rates for women and people of colour.[42] These statistics highlight the need for increased awareness and action to address AI biases, ensuring fairness and equal opportunities in employment for all individuals. Efforts are being made to develop more transparent and accountable AI systems, implement rigorous testing and validation processes, and promote diverse and inclusive data sets to mitigate biases in AI technology. Again, I will return to look at how to mitigate AI bias in Chapter Six, and what it means to build AI that is both trustworthy and trusted.

Summary

In this chapter I have moved away from the theoretical to begin the practical planning of an AI strategy for your business. I began by showing you how to properly assess your organisation's readiness for AI by looking at your current propensity for agility, trust, customer orientation and innovation. I also explored how to build an integrated strategy with an overarching vision that is embedded into your business strategy, before talking about the importance that your people hold. I established that your internal talent is a critical piece of the puzzle if you want to see long-term success in your AI projects, and that you need to work hard to attract that talent.

FIVE
Achieving Competitive Advantage Through AI

In this chapter I'll give you the practical steps to put in place to use AI in a way that unlocks value and gives you long-term benefit. I'll look at the key steps on the roadmap towards AI implementation, including goal-setting and how to decide which initiatives to undertake and the way to inform and engage your stakeholders in them. I'll also discuss your data infrastructure and what key assets you need to have considered or have in place before you begin collecting data for your AI outputs. Then I'll turn to the three areas in which I have seen AI successfully transform business – operational efficiency, customer experience and decision-making – before finally giving advice on how to monitor the progress of your initiatives to ensure you're getting the best outcomes.

Your roadmap to implementing AI

You've assessed your readiness, considered an integrated strategy and recruited, engaged and manoeuvred the right talent to work towards successfully implementing AI in your organisation. Next, it's time to put in place a roadmap for your AI programme that will help you to gain competitive advantage. It's this roadmap that will make sure you tackle the right projects in the optimum places and achieve ROI quickly.

The first step of this process is to audit your organisation to identify the areas in which AI can have the greatest impact. Look at the AI applications that could impact or streamline your processes across operations, sales, marketing, customer service and the supply chain. With ongoing developments in the AI landscape, developing a team of enthusiasts who can scan the horizon for new tech and opportunities to implement AI will ensure you stay current.

Engineer value

Extracting value from your digital and AI projects begins with understanding where value lies. When introducing AI tools, a common initial mistake businesses make is not deciding what meaningful and relevant value looks like in advance. This means beginning by deciding on your strategic business initiatives. These need to be:

- Critical to your business success in the short and/or medium term
- Actionable and measurable with a financial goal (eg reduce, increase, optimise)
- Time-bound with a clear delivery time frame
- Cross-functional or cross-departmental
- Owned by a senior internal stakeholder
- Documented and communicated

These initiatives are often found in annual reports, on company websites, in press releases or as part of annual executive conference presentations. They are aspirational and speak to the future drive, direction and momentum of the organisation. They don't speak to specific technologies, such as moving your video meeting technology from Zoom to Microsoft Teams or transitioning from desktop to laptop PCs. Instead, they talk about the financially measurable initiatives – things that will impact the way in which your company derives value. This might be through its operations, sales and marketing or customer relationships. For example:

- Improving customer lifetime value by retaining more customers for longer
- Improving supply chain quality and reliability
- Reducing unplanned downtime and improving maintenance times and effectiveness

- Reducing inventory costs
- Improving cash flow positioning by reducing the lead-to-sales cycle timeframe

Your strategic business initiatives are ways to re-engineer your ability to bring value into the business. These often simply boil down to things like 'optimising operational efficiency' or 'creating new opportunities for revenue'; where you can, you should make them specific to your business in its current context.

Create objectives and key results

Once you have defined your strategic business initiatives with your leadership team, it is time to decide on and understand the company's short-, medium- and long-term goals, then build a framework, such as objectives and key results (OKRs), around them.

This framework will help to ensure that your initiatives focus on positively impacting company performance. OKRs use goal-setting with SMART success criteria to make sure the way your strategy is executed links and contributes to your company goals. This then allows you to enhance performance over time.

The aim is to use this framework to create an environment where there is high engagement with and a focus on continuous improvement, and where there is the flexibility and autonomy to experiment and innovate in a way that is connected to the overall purpose of your business.

Work with your team to tie together your objectives and a meaningful way of measuring them. This way, you can be sure that you're accurately assessing your achievement. Your objectives may have multiple key results attached to them. These can be qualitative or quantitative measures, which helps to give a complete view of the impact of your transformation project.

For example, if your objective is to grow your business to achieve global reach, your key results might be:

- Launching two products in EMEA
- Building an online brand presence in the US
- Growing revenue to £5 million in the US
- Growing revenue to £7 million in EMEA

If your objective is to become a fully environmentally sustainable business, your key results might be:

- Auditing the supply chain for sustainable partners
- Reaching net zero on all exports and imports
- Creating fully carbon-neutral offices

The adapted version of this OKRs framework, to which I have become accustomed in my work and which is also used by Google, enables teams to work collaboratively across the usual departmental silos that exist within organisations. It helps to address the issue of soft skills through formal training initiatives and 'learn by doing' scenarios.

Objectives are set for each cycle, and key results are defined. These are inspirational, qualitative goals that are obtainable within a quarter and represent the shared imagination of the team.

By aligning your digital initiatives and the everyday tasks of your teams to the OKRs you've set around AI, you will ensure everyone is working towards common goals. Make sure these team-level OKRs contribute to and work towards the company-wide key objectives (which will always drive into the vision of your business). When teams know the organisation's goals and vision, they can effectively set their OKRs, which helps maintain motivation. This collaborative effort to set and achieve goals is directly linked to employee engagement and satisfaction, contributing to a culture of purpose, growth and autonomy.

Decide on your AI initiatives

Look, first, for the quick wins – easy-to-implement, low-cost solutions that can act as use cases to prove the value of AI to the wider company. These will often be those that carry out manual, repetitive tasks that are susceptible to human error and act as a drain on employees' time. You can identify these by engaging with your employees and asking them where they feel their time is most often wasted.

This will have two key benefits: first, you'll get your information direct from the frontline, so you'll address the real, day-to-day problems your workforce encounters. Second, you'll engage your employees right from the beginning of the project, showing them that AI will be used to make their lives easier and their jobs more enjoyable.

Line these initiatives up with your strategic business initiatives. It's OK to start small. This might mean implementing AI tech to take and record the minutes for meetings and emailing all attendees with a summary and key action points, or it might mean bringing AI into your sales process to improve your customer relationship management, identify churn risks, highlight buying patterns or provide personality insights.

Once you've identified these opportunities, anchor them to your strategic business initiatives. If an AI initiative does not fit with your business strategy, then put it to one side and move on to those that do.

Inform

Once you have your vision in place, the next step is to inform stakeholders of the potential merits of using AI across the business. This will increase buy-in even further. It doesn't have to be a complicated endeavour.

A regular newsletter will create an opportunity to keep stakeholders up to date with the industry and latest uses of AI, both in the business and the wider sector. It could be the catalyst for a working group to discuss relevant developments and collect new ideas for AI business applications. These will work together to scan the horizon for new opportunities for digital and AI. Furthermore, the working group will identify training needs and invite guest speakers to increase awareness and understanding.

An effective working group requires a 'boots on the ground' approach. Members need to be representative of all levels of the business to avoid an 'ivory tower' – the perception that decisions are being made in isolation, from the top, without real engagement with or consideration for those who will be delivering. Engaging people across the organisation will ensure the group has diversity of thought and a wide-ranging, positive business impact.

In many ways, businesses are like an extensive social network in the way people interact with one another. Because of this, the working group and regular newsletter will raise awareness and create a positive narrative through a network of influencers to reach the key stakeholders.

If the company has a shared information board, such as an intranet, post regular updates and spotlight the team members involved in the projects to help create buzz around the activities.

Engage

Once a dialogue about the potential applications of AI has been opened within the business, use the roadmap to work with engaged stakeholders, and start to address the internal challenges.

Next, identify the priorities of those stakeholders and work with them to engage with the areas they are passionate about. Assign them a challenge which aligns to their area of interest. As they engage with the newsletter and working group, solicit ideas and feedback from them as to where value can be added or inefficiencies reduced. Use these as a starting point for exploring appropriate digital AI tools. As your key stakeholders see that the project is led by business requirements (including their own), they will lend further support and become champions of the improvement cycle.

Develop the benefits case

Use the links with your key stakeholders to develop the benefits case for each initiative. This could be done in a one-to-one scenario or as part of the wider working group. As you develop those benefits, consider these four points:

1. Go back to the strategic business initiatives and link the AI benefits to the business outcomes.

2. Make sure, wherever possible, that the business outcomes rely on the success of the AI project.

3. Assign each AI initiative a key stakeholder who will champion the project across the business and work with teams to instigate the culture change necessary for acceptance.

4. Identify the disadvantages that could result in objections from the wider business and use both the business plan and your engaged stakeholders to answer these.

Once you have achieved these steps, the next step is to bring the implementation of AI to life with a prototype. Ensure that the visual elements of the prototype are high impact and use the prototype to iron out any remaining objections and identify flaws or issues.

Building data infrastructure

Data infrastructure – the foundation of AI – refers to the methods, means and mechanisms involved with data. These are:

- Collection and integration
- Storage and management
- Processing and analysis

Getting these operations right is crucial if you want your AI implementation to be successful in the long term. The larger and more accurate your pool of data, the better your AI outputs and analyses will be.

Creating a comprehensive infrastructure is the first step to ensuring you're collecting accurate data, storing it compliantly and processing it in such ways that AI systems are empowered to deliver useful information, insights and predictions. A strong data infrastructure enables businesses to harness the power of AI and make data-driven decisions, move more quickly than the competition and gain a competitive edge in the market. In this section I will guide you through the three key steps involved in building a robust data infrastructure.

Data collection and integration

AI relies on a large amount of high-quality data, and the more accurate and complete your data is, the better the AI output will be. That means one of the first steps in your AI implementation roadmap is to establish an effective data collection process. Your process should identify relevant data sources and define your data types. Then, once you have this process in place, selecting the right integration tools will set you in good stead for successful AI implementation.

A good place to start is by looking at all the different entry points you have available for data collection.

This might be email newsletters, social media adverts, in-person events, sales or other user interactions and metadata sources. Take stock of all the different data types you collect and how each can be used – whether it's to give you better insight, improve your customer journey, increase your personalisation or encourage sales.

All this data then needs to be integrated from its various sources into an infrastructure that can sort and learn from it.

Data storage and management

That infrastructure needs to be able to store all the collected data securely. Security and accessibility are critical factors in building a comprehensive data infrastructure. Choosing the right storage system, defining data retention policies, and implementing data backup and recovery procedures are essential steps in ensuring both the integrity and availability of your data.

This may be cloud or physical server storage – it will depend on your situation as to which is right for you. There's a tendency to think of physical, on-site storage (known as local storage) as the more secure option but this isn't necessarily the case.

Secure cloud storage with well-defined access controls and regular backup protocols can ensure the security of your data without the responsibility of managing and maintaining the network, servers and infrastructure. Whatever data storage option you choose must be reliable, scalable and efficient.

Data processing and analysis

The timely and accurate processing and analysis of data is key to unlocking the full potential of AI. This step enables businesses to make data-driven decisions and improve the accuracy of predictive models. Selecting the right processing and analysis tools, defining data-processing workflows and performing data quality checks are pivotal in this process.

By following these concrete actions and leveraging relevant examples of best practice, your business can build a comprehensive data infrastructure that forms the backbone of successful AI implementation. Embracing change and innovation in this digital age is vital; with the right strategy and tools, your business can seize the opportunities provided by AI and position itself as a leader in your industry. The journey towards AI-powered success begins with a solid data infrastructure – the foundation for the transformation that lies ahead.

Three categories of AI initiatives

The AI initiatives that could have an impact on your business fall broadly into three categories.

Increasing operational efficiency

Projects that can increase your operational efficiency are ones that will streamline your processes, eliminate low-skilled, time-consuming tasks and automate repetitive or data-intensive work. In sales this might mean using AI for data input, lead discovery and lead scoring, speeding up the legwork required before relationship building can begin.

In sectors such as manufacturing, logistics and facilities management, predictive maintenance is saving companies time and money by using data analytics to understand equipment and machinery usage and intercepting issues before they arise. Similarly, AI-powered predictive models are being used in finance and cybersecurity to analyse large volumes of data to identify trends and patterns associated with fraud. ML algorithms are uncovering hidden relationships and indicators that human analysts may miss. Predictive analytics can help in identifying potential fraud cases based on historical data and ongoing transactions.

Achieving operational efficiency through digital tools doesn't necessarily come from replacing humans. Rather, this is about helping to ensure that human resources are being used in the most cost-effective way. Company-wide digital transformation is an opportunity to highlight where there are process inefficiencies and find digital solutions to them. AI is one tool in the toolbox to do this, but, crucially, it's the way this tool interacts with and is used by the employees on the ground that will lead to success.

AI requires a symbiotic relationship with humans. It can play one of five roles:

1. **Automator:** This is where most AI is currently being used. This is low-stakes decision-making in areas where AI has all the context and a conclusion needs to be reached quickly. In these scenarios – think personalised marketing, dynamic pricing, automated display ads – AI can decide the outcome and implement it without human intervention. The data can be fed in, and a relatively safe outcome can be pulled out.

2. **Decider:** This is where we've begun to see AI break through over the past twelve months. AI is being used as a resource to help humans complete tasks more quickly. AI acts as a decider when it has plenty of context, but the execution still requires humans – for example, with predictive maintenance. AI can identify the issue or the answer, but humans are still needed for implementation.

3. **Recommender:** AI can also act as a trusted partner to experts. When there are multiple, repetitive decisions to be made but the full data is not available, or qualitative considerations

need to be considered, AI can recommend optimum paths or suggestions and humans can decide which to follow.

4. **Illuminator:** There are times when inherently creative work can benefit from a data-driven approach, and in these cases ML can improve on the human output. For example, in product design, running designs through ML tools that layer on a range of customer preference data can lead to a product outcome that is more closely aligned to the desires of the largest possible target audience. In these cases, humans can leverage AI-generated insights within the creative process.

5. **Evaluator:** Finally, when there's not enough context and the stakes are high, AI should not be left to generate or make decisions. In situations where human empathy is required and the needs of many individuals must be considered, or when human psychology can impact decision-making in areas such as layout planning or seasonal promotions for a store, humans should generate scenarios which AI can then evaluate.

Only the first of these roles (AI acting as an automator) can be performed without human input, but for AI to be a transformative tool for organisations, it needs to move beyond automation and focus on generating, learning and scaling.

Enhancing customer experience

By 2025 AI identification of customer emotions will influence 30% of the messaging they receive digitally.[43] Emotional intelligence is a crucial element of customer experience, but understanding the sentiment of a conversation is much harder when it is taking place virtually. AI sentiment analysis is now beginning to analyse, process and respond to user emotions in the following ways:

- Natural language analysis looks at speech and text to find patterns and trends that suggest the sentiment of the words.

- Computer-vision facial expression analysis looks for facial patterns in response to stimuli.

- Speech analysis detects emotional states combined with facial muscle movements and body language.

- Biometric sensors monitor heart rate, eye movement and physical movement in response to stimuli.

This is part of a raft of AI tools being developed that will vastly improve its ability to personalise the customer experience. It will give more detailed relationship intelligence to help segment customers, recommend products, offer dynamic pricing and guide conversations.

In the retail industry, businesses can create intelligent experience engines, powered by AI and customer data, to optimise every touchpoint across all channels. This approach enables businesses to offer more personalised customer experiences, which can lead to revenue increases and larger sales. AI personalisation can also help design targeted marketing strategies, boosting customer engagement and ROI.

For the financial services sector, the use of AI-driven personalisation is crucial. It can help institutions manage business costs, deliver omnichannel experiences and foster a culture of innovation. AI-powered personalisation can improve the digital banking experience by recognising customers and offering personalised services and relevant suggestions based on customer behaviour. This leads to increased customer loyalty and efficiency.

AI also plays a significant role in enhancing marketing efforts across all industries. By analysing customer data, AI can help businesses understand customer behaviour and preferences, leading to more effective marketing strategies and campaigns and thereby increasing sales and revenue.

Improving decision-making

Once you've determined which data and data types will be needed for your projects (text, voice, image, audio, video), your data management and engineering team need to source the collection points and turn that data into actionable insights. When they've mapped all the places data is being collected, they can then build solutions to enable that data collection. This means evaluating the existing data collection points across the company, and any new potential points of entry. Use these to map out the ML models to help you reach your business objectives.

Next, you need to collect and sort relevant, trusted and fresh internal and external data, information and information types. Any AI solution you implement needs a continuous stream of high-quality, relevant data to perform properly. Data engineers should use real-time and batch processing to ensure that AI solutions have constant input, while enabling governance policies to address the necessary regulatory and security concerns.

With AI, more data is better and it's important that data is properly sorted for context. Data engineers should curate, label and certify data using automation-focused ML tools. These tools will automate repetitive and time-intensive tasks, enabling your data scientists to build models, iterate faster, try more features and algorithms, and tackle higher-priority projects.

Collected data can then be prepared for sharing, and tested and trained for code quality and bias. As a result, you'll be deploying solutions that are based on real-time, accurate data that gives you clear insight into the needs of the business and your customers.

In HR and recruitment, this can transform hiring processes through accurate job fit scoring and candidate ranking, as well as improve retention by better understanding your employee sentiments. In retail, this can give insight into your most profitable customers and their lifetime value, and inform real-time price optimisation.

Measuring and monitoring progress

As you set up your initiatives, don't forget to consider how you plan to monitor their ongoing value and measure their success. Having a clear idea of what to measure before you start will help you gain appropriate snapshots of value throughout the project, and you will get the clearest picture of overall success. Just as importantly, it will make it easier to document and learn from mistakes and failures. You're likely to experience at least some failure if you're undertaking large AI initiatives, and in itself this isn't an issue. See these experiences as more helpful data to set you on course for your goals. According to research done by Boston Consulting Group, companies that track their progress against clear goals are 74% more likely to succeed than those who don't, but in a large organisation it can be hard to know where to start.[44]

Quantifying the expected outcomes is the crucial first step for ensuring the effort is targeting true areas of value. Do this before you start – even if these outcomes change, it's important to have a starting point to help you decide on your direction.

Tracking progress is the next step – 75% of successful transformations have effective monitoring and data analytics.[45] Proper monitoring enables 50% improvement in dynamic adjustment of financing throughout the transformation.[46]

A strong central department, such as a transformation management office, will improve monitoring by making sure someone is responsible for tracking metrics. Reporting is more effective when it starts with a trusted reporting entity with a clear remit who can challenge leaders, track progress and hold people accountable for delivering against set targets. Metrics should be simple, clear and critical, and directly tied to the strategic intent of the project and the business outcomes. All the targets put in place should have a person or a team directly accountable for delivery against that target.

Finally (and most crucially), there should be a single source of truth for data, as this enables businesses to resolve issues such as baselines, net vs gross benefits and double-counting. All operational and finance data should marry up.

The following considerations will help you find success in your measurement:

- **Progress monitoring:** Set up initiatives for success by assigning specific business owners and having a clear understanding of the starting point.

- **Minimise the burden on the organisation:** Tracking should be simple and automated, wherever possible. It makes sense to keep things manageable so the tracking gets done, rather than creating something overly complex that ends up falling by the wayside.

- **Empower data owners:** They need to be able to call out impediments to progress, so give them the ability to identify the blockers. Tracking is a means to push the transformation forward, so ensure there is full transparency of what needs to be fixed and allow data collection to focus on resolving issues. Where blocks exist, see them as a request for help.

Effective monitoring of results is the only way to show real ROI, and it's ROI-based performance that will enable the project to continue with momentum and support from the right people. Choose your north star metric – that might be purchases, it might be downloads, it might be volume, it might be active users. It's the thing that denotes how many happy customers you have based on how they usually behave.

Summary

After showing you how to assess your readiness, in Chapter Five I have laid the groundwork for putting in place your roadmap for AI. I looked specifically at ways to extract value from your AI projects by tying them to your strategic business initiatives and establishing a framework for measurement, such as OKRs. With all these foundations secure, I then went through the steps you should take to set your AI strategy in motion: informing your stakeholders, engaging with your people, developing a benefits case and building a robust data infrastructure. I then categorised AI initiatives into three distinct benefit areas, with examples – operational efficiency, customer experience and decision-making – and concluded by giving advice on how to measure the progress of your initiatives against your goals.

SIX
Overcoming Challenges And Mitigating Risks

In this chapter I'll explore in more detail the challenges and risks that have been raised so far in this book, and equip you with practical tools for overcoming them. I'll consider common cultural, technical and regulatory issues that you may face, and discuss a process to put in place to mitigate the risks of using generative AI that has yet to be regulated. Next, I'll discuss the critical role that business leaders play in successfully deploying AI across their organisations. Finally, I'll return to the topics of data privacy and bias.

Cultural, technical and regulatory hurdles

Challenges exist at every stage of the AI adoption journey that often require expert advice to navigate. I've already looked at ways to assess company readiness for those who have not yet begun their AI implementation journey, but even companies with established AI programs may find, as the capabilities of generative AI continue to increase, that the governance and frameworks they have in place need adjusting. Adopting AI comes with multiple hurdles – both internal and external.

Internally, companies will need to navigate their existing employee culture. This may mean breaking down silos, addressing fears, upskilling, redeploying talent, creating new processes and adjusting communication methods. Having key stakeholders in place across different departments who can act as champions and early adopters will help to smooth out and speed up this process.

There are external pressures to consider too. Trust needs to be built between companies and their customers, and misusing AI can damage this relationship. It's crucial to think carefully about how your AI projects may affect the way you interact with your customers and the impact this might have on them and their perception of your business.

With so many hurdles to clear, having a plan in place to mitigate risk is important. Different types of AI come with different risks, but generative AI seems to be gaining traction most quickly inside the workplace. Here are five best-practice principles

OVERCOMING CHALLENGES AND MITIGATING RISKS

I suggest following when implementing generative AI-powered projects:

1. **Test everything:** For any new AI tool you're looking to implement, start by setting up a test for it internally and run it through your employee base first. Whether it's internal reports, meeting summaries, product imagery or explainer videos, look for employee use cases first. If you're introducing a chatbot for customer service, set it up for an internal department. For example, divert all employee IT queries through the chatbot, and do extensive testing with your internal stakeholders before introducing anything externally. This will help you to assess the positive and negative reactions you're likely to get from customers, as well as identify and resolve any usage or capability issues.

2. **Respect privacy:** Another growing concern with AI is data protection and privacy. Many are calling for AI usage to slow down while data protection regulation catches up. Again, it's crucial to have robust policies around how AI will use and handle sensitive data. If identifying data is going to be input into an LLM, procedures for protecting and deleting that data need to be in place before it is used by the public. Ensure your data protection policy is updated to include data input into or output from AI tools.

3. **Set up guard rails:** Bias and accuracy are two of the most pervasive issues with any generative AI tool, as the outputs are only ever as good as the data being fed in. You need to have a system in place that can identify inaccuracies that occur or any bias that might be magnified. LLMs need considerable fine-tuning, so pair any LLM tools with agent-based modelling to improve their accuracy and enhance their contextual understanding. Have policies in place for the use of generative AI and LLMs and try to ensure that any outputs have a subject matter expert on hand to fact-check and identify bias.

4. **Be transparent:** Never attempt to pass off AI as human. If someone is going to encounter a chatbot, whether it's staff, customers, clients or other stakeholders, make sure they're aware they're going to be interacting with AI. Being honest with people will help to diffuse the issues of mistrust that already exist around AI. Ultimately, trying to pass AI off as human, no matter how sophisticated the tool, will erode trust.

5. **Beta for longer:** When you do take an AI tool to the public, soft-launch it in beta mode for further testing. While you may want to rush out a launch of a new AI tool or feature, remember that beta can be your best friend when experimenting with new tech. Keep new features in beta for longer than you might normally to manage expectations, gather feedback and give you time

to identify and fix bugs. If the tool is still in beta when an error or issue arises, users are more likely to be understanding (and forgiving) if something doesn't work as it should.

Following these five steps will help to address most of the technical and regulatory challenges you're likely to encounter, but, as I've already identified, the largest barrier to digital change in most organisations is a cultural one. Cultural challenges need to be addressed with a different set of considerations, and one of the most important is a strong, involved leadership team.

Companies with a strong commitment from effective leaders – the CEO down to middle management – are more likely to succeed in their AI projects. There are two key problems that need to be solved here, which I will discuss in the following paragraphs.

Visible commitment and leadership from the CEO

The organisations that meet or exceed their targets for digital transformation are the ones that have CEOs checking in at least quarterly with the progress of projects to help steer the effort. In research they recently carried out across their client base, the Boston Consulting Group found that over 90% of the companies who have succeeded had digital transformation on the CEO or board agenda.[47]

This means it's crucial that the leader and key executives have a high profile and active role in communicating the importance of the transformation. They should be seen as driving the initiatives, meeting with the transformation team regularly to support them and resolve any issues that arise. Senior leaders should participate in frequent, forensic reviews of progress, and they should be seen by the whole business giving regular updates on this progress with enthusiasm and purpose. In a nutshell, they should aim for these three things:

1. Leaders must rethink how to engage and create excitement about the transformation.
2. Leaders must demonstrate compassion and care – lay-offs, reskilling and redeployment are inevitable.
3. Leaders must be agile and ready to make bold decisions to drive commitment, and be open to reassessing the vison and changing the leadership.

Motivate and empower middle management

Engaging with middle management can be tough – often they don't buy into the transformation because their goals and incentives are not aligned with the digital transformation efforts. It's crucial to get the 'frozen middle' on board to lead their teams and embed the principles day-to-day. Middle managers should be involved early in the process, developing the objectives, business cases and approach to transformation, and helping to make these relevant for their team/business area.

Make sure middle managers have the support, information and tools in place to cascade the same messages to their teams. Link their performance objectives to the success of the digital transformation and take a head-on approach to rewarding those who become champions of digital progress, while sidelining people who act as blockers.

Finally, make sure that mentoring and feedback are provided to middle managers to help them understand the impact of the digital initiatives and empower them to lead change. Purpose motivates people, so ensuring they know the purpose and buy into the vision is crucial.

Ensuring data privacy and security

The cultural resistance to AI is only one of the challenges that businesses need to overcome in AI adoption. Another persistent concern is data privacy and security. As AI increasingly drives business processes and ML consumes more and more data, businesses are scrambling to find ways of ensuring they aren't breaching data protection laws. The extensive, pervasive collection and use of personal data as a commodity input has been named 'surveillance capitalism' and it has widespread social implications.[48] Privacy infringements far beyond the 'user's perceived norms of privacy' – browsing history, location tracking, facial and voice data – occurring without user knowledge or consent threaten the bond of trust between business and consumer.[49] This behavioural data is being used by organisations to predict and influence customer behaviour though hyper-personalisation, or even 'micro-manipulations' such as 'first-degree price discrimination' – selling products at the exact price point each customer is willing to pay.[50]

All of this is leading to the erosion of the social fabric that drives constructive and healthy discourse and societal relationships. Echo chambers, political polarisation, extremism, widespread confusion and mistrust caused by mis- and disinformation are all resulting features of reinforcement loops designed to increase engagement and economic gain. These loops are specifically created to feed users information that strengthens existing beliefs rather than helping to balance views. As a result, we're seeing a huge impact on mental health, autonomy, reason, constructive communication, and agency.[51]

In addition, collecting and processing vast amounts of data in this way poses considerable security risks. Risk of data breaches, cyberattacks and mishandling of personal information are all increased. Each of these can erode trust in public institutions and private corporations, which has political implications. Mass audience manipulation and lobbying by large organisations in concentrated markets is already a tactic we've seen played out in recent years because of the 'winner takes all' nature of digital technologies. This has enabled global companies to make power grabs, furthering economic inequalities and even mass unemployment. The impact has been the erosion of local community development and economies as tax revenues have moved across sovereign borders. This stifles technological innovation because smaller and more diverse organisations cease to exist as markets become increasingly concentrated.

Safeguarding the use of data is critical to maintain the social, economic and political balance that is currently being outpaced by technological innovation. Access to AI tools has been rapidly democratised without the necessary time to focus on privacy concerns and the laws surrounding them. There are currently no proper controls on what data is put into these tools, and neither is there any transparency around what data is used for training LLMs or what (potentially sensitive) data is retained by them. As such, there remain serious questions around the compliance of these AI (and specifically generative AI) tools.

To move past these concerns, organisations must find ways to exercise thoughtful analysis of the data sets they are using with AI tools to prepare training data that is controlled, compliant and auditable. There is a myriad of challenges with AI regulation, as the concerns touch social, technological, economic, environmental and political (STEEP) externalities, and regulators and policymakers will want to balance the need for regulation with the benefits of innovation.

This may mean adopting a combination of private market solutions (giving equal access to enabling technologies) alongside a simple regulatory framework (such as proportionate funding distribution). By tackling the issue this way, the variety that is needed for high-quality tech innovation can still be achieved while avoiding the hyper-concentrated markets that commonly lead to disproportionate power accumulation.[52] Local enforcement of a simple regulatory framework is more likely to succeed than detailed regulation accounting for individual STEEP externalities, because the local impact will vary significantly.

Fairness concerns and mitigating bias

Bias risks are one of the key arguments for AI and ML not replacing humans in the decision-making process, and the concern surrounding bias in AI has risen almost as quickly as the tools themselves. This is unsurprising considering those who have been burnt by algorithmic bias have suffered lost revenue, reduced customer loyalty, difficulty hiring the best talent or higher rates of attrition as a result. Despite this, in a 2020 study on AI and ML, only 24% of respondents reported unbiased, diverse, global AI as mission-critical.[53]

Fairness in decision-making is a complex topic, but what's imperative is that AI is trustworthy, trusted and explainable. There is an assumption that AI is intrinsically unbiased and that it can intervene to improve decision-making where human bias exists. However, ML models are written by humans and trained on data generated and chosen by humans. For the time being at least, ML techniques boil down to pattern recognition. They are prediction machines. Any human biases underlying or built into the models will likely lead them to amplify these in their predictions. Successful ML models are predicated on good-quality data. This means data that is:

- Complete
- Available and accessible
- Current and relevant
- Accurate
- Valid
- Usable and interpretable
- Reliable and credible[54]

Where there are trade-offs in the quality of training data, outputs are less accurate and/or magnify existing biases in the text. If there is an over-reliance on the ML algorithm for decision-making, and human judgement and accountability are removed from the process, issues will occur. As AI tools repeat existing social and cultural norms and biases, they are codified. Due to the speed at which ML models identify patterns and make predictions, these biases are repeated, reinforced and amplified. The consequences of poor data are compounded as errors and biased outputs are then re-consumed as inputs.

A recent survey shows respondents reporting bias in AI algorithms contributing to gender discrimination (32%), age discrimination (32%), racial discrimination (29%), sexual orientation discrimination (19%) and religious discrimination (18%).[55]

Modern ML techniques are designed to improve performance by consuming larger training data sets, making 'explainability' challenging. During the development and testing phases, algorithmic bias and errors are harder to identify, increasing the risk of adverse consequences in production systems.

Building responsible AI

To be responsible in your use of AI, and to mitigate the risks associated with AI bias, you'll need to take a proactive approach to monitoring your AI training data and models. This means, at the most basic level, looking for outliers in your data, and comparing and validating your training data to ensure it is representative, diverse and as bias-free as possible. You can do this by following these steps:

1. Initially it's important that you're not trying to tackle too many scenarios with your AI algorithm. This would require an unmanageable number of labels and classes. Try to narrow down the business problem you want to solve and create as specific a definition of it as you can manage. Creating a use case that is narrow and specific will help you to assess how well your model is performing its task.

2. As you gather data for input, find ways to ensure you're gathering a wide range of differing opinions and viewpoints. There is often more than one valid opinion for a data point. Making space for diversity of opinion and legitimate disagreements will create a more flexible and inclusive model.

3. Don't feed in training data that you haven't already combed through. You need to understand your data and know all its different classifications and categories, plus all the different labels that will sit inside those classes. By taking ownership of these, and seeing where your training data fits, you'll be less likely

to get surprising or objectionable biases in the output.

4. Another way to avoid bias in your ML outputs is to ensure that your data science and data engineering teams are diverse, come from a range of different backgrounds and bring different experiences and opinions to the table so they can ask diverse questions of the AI model. Look for diversity in race, gender, age, experience, socio-economic background, culture and sexuality, as this will bring a wider range of questions and interactions with the model.

5. Build with your end users in mind. They too will be different from you and from your team, not least because there's a likelihood that they will have a lot less experience interacting with AI and similar technology. Be empathetic, undertake research to understand the problems they are looking to solve, and put yourself in their shoes to interact with your model. This will help you identify the problems that may arise for less tech-savvy audiences.

6. Use human annotators throughout your training and retraining. Human annotators quality-check your data and are trained to spot details and mistakes. Make sure that your pool of annotators bring with them a diversity of viewpoints, and use more than one in your training cycle. This will reduce bias both as you launch your model and then as you retrain your annotators. Human

annotators are more accurate and efficient than automated ones, so they'll not only reduce bias but they'll also reduce overall cost.

7. Gather feedback at every stage from as many users as you can. Test repeatedly and, as I have suggested previously, use a longer beta phase to your advantage. When you deploy your model, do so with avenues for user feedback so you can understand how the model is working in real-world scenarios. This might be a simple feedback form, individual user interviews or a larger forum. Gathering this feedback will help you to ensure that your released models are performing in the way you expected.

8. Finally, once you've gathered that feedback, make sure you have a concrete plan in place to use the feedback to make improvements. You need to be constantly iterating your model to improve its performance and accuracy, so use client feedback and independent auditing for changes, edge cases (these are scenarios the algorithm hasn't encountered before and can crop up in real-world usage) or any instances of bias that might have been missed in the initial training. Inputting this feedback into the model will help to improve its outputs.

It's also worth adding here that a crucial step in avoiding bias across AI is to be honest with ourselves about the extent of our own bias. This means understanding that, no matter how broad a view we may feel we have, when we engage with AI, and generative AI in particular, we all need to accept that we will have blind spots and 'preferences' which will lead to both conscious and unconscious biases showing up in the results.

Building responsible AI requires transparency and humility. There must be a drive for continuous improvement. You could start by putting in place a code of conduct or ethical guidelines around your AI training and execution. Make sure there is tight governance around your AI initiatives and, where you can, standardise the processes, reporting, and optimisation techniques.

I've already addressed company culture as a challenge, but it's worth stating again that culture is crucial to AI success, not only in adopting AI but also in encouraging and prioritising ethical practices and procedures. Create safe spaces for people to voice their concerns and ask questions. Be transparent with team members and help them to feel ownership of the transformation taking place.

Summary

In this chapter my focus has shifted to considering some of the challenges, risks and objections that are commonly put forward around AI. Both internal and external challenges exist. Internally, there's a need for cultural transformation within organisations, which includes dismantling silos, upskilling employees and implementing new processes. Externally, companies face pressures around trust and relationship management with customers, and thoughtful AI project consideration is crucial to mitigate negative impacts on customer interactions and perceptions.

I proposed five best-practice principles for implementing generative AI, and then I explained why commitment from leadership is pivotal to AI project success. Active and visible involvement from CEOs and well-engaged middle management are essential. The alignment of middle management goals with transformation efforts, coupled with adequate support, information and motivation, can significantly influence the project's outcome.

Finally, I spent time considering data privacy and bias. With the extensive collection of behavioural data for hyper-personalisation and micro-manipulations, we have seen a rise in societal impacts like echo chambers, misinformation, political polarisation and poor mental health. Responsible use of AI is critical if it's going to be a feasible solution in the long term.

SEVEN
The Future Of AI In Organisations

The past couple of chapters have shown you how to build a roadmap for the implementation of AI in your business – one that considers your internal and external stakeholders and gives you quick wins that build momentum for larger AI projects.

AI has undeniably altered the landscape of business. From predictive analytics to customer service automation, AI continues to redefine how businesses operate, compete and innovate. In the near future, I anticipate even more groundbreaking shifts catalysed by AI, making it essential for business leaders to understand and adapt to these emerging trends.

In this chapter I'll explore the trends that are likely to dominate the conversations around AI over the coming years. I'll look at issues such as the democratisation of AI, hyper-automation, human–AI collaboration and regulatory frameworks. Then I'll look at how you can stay competitive for the long term in a marketplace that is constantly shifting and among consumers whose expectations are rapidly expanding. Finally, I'll give you an overview of how to stay resilient in the era of AI.

The next frontier of AI in business

Though I certainly don't have a crystal ball, I can predict some growth areas for AI over the next five years: the areas of life it will influence, the ways in which it will be used, and the most common applications area already being seen in smaller use cases across the globe. I'll explore some of these and see what they may mean for business leaders wanting to position themselves to make the best use of AI in the coming years.

Democratisation of AI

In 2023 we saw a seismic shift in both the use and the availability of AI. No longer a tool for the exclusive use of tech giants and corporations, AI has already become far more accessible than most would have imagined even just twelve months beforehand. There are four main ways AI is being democratised:

THE FUTURE OF AI IN ORGANISATIONS

1. Probably the most obvious form of democratisation is that usage and access have spread with advancements in cloud-based AI services. With tools like ChatGPT, Bard, Stable Diffusion and Synthesia available for all, small and medium-sized enterprises now have the same access to innovative generative tools as larger organisations. This broad accessibility will level the playing field, enabling more businesses to benefit from AI applications.

2. Another form of democratisation is in AI development. There is considerable excitement around the fact that a wider range of people can contribute to the design and development of new AI tools and applications. The more diverse the development of these contributors is, the more innovative and diverse the tools they create will be. This is being done in two ways: through making tools open-source, which means anyone can download the model (agreeing to terms of use) and then modify it themselves; but also, and more crucially, AI development is democratised by making it easier for people with minimal programming experience and little familiarity with ML to participate, using 'no code' tools to build models.

3. Further democratisation comes via the benefits of AI – facilitating the broad and equitable distribution of benefits to communities that build, control and adopt advanced AI

capabilities. If the bulk of the value and the benefits of AI go to a minority of large corporations, then true democratisation hasn't occurred. Some are arguing (the CTO of Microsoft included) that the wealth created through AI should be invested in and redistributed across communities, enabling and encouraging further innovation.

4. Over the coming years, we'll also see the democratisation of governance. Governance decisions are about balancing risk and reward to determine how AI should be used, developed and disseminated, and who should be involved in that process. Governance often goes hand in hand with influence, which means those who are governing decisions around the use and development of AI are influencing a wider community of users and stakeholders. Democratising this governance addresses concerns that tech companies hold too much control over where technology is going, how it's used and what constitutes safe, responsible development and distribution.

For business owners, AI democratisation means the opportunity to have more influence in the AI landscape, the tools being created, their governance and their use. With potential ownership of and engagement with AI models comes a greater drive to train and upskill employees to build and use AI tools. Integrating AI across your business operations will be

THE FUTURE OF AI IN ORGANISATIONS

more feasible than ever. Start by identifying key areas of your operations that could benefit from automation or data analytics. Then explore available AI solutions that meet your needs. Hire or train talent with the skills to help these projects succeed.

Hyper-automated processes

One of the most exciting opportunities AI offers is the ability to integrate multiple tools and technologies and have them all automated in response to valuable operational data that businesses have been collecting for years. This takes the process of automation we've seen emerging over the past decade a step further to what has become known as hyper-automation. AI will not only automate routine tasks but also high-level, complex tasks thanks to advancements in ML and NLP.

Unlike typical automation, hyper-automation allows us to access and integrate complex operational data like customer service interactions, shipping logistics, sentiment scores and analytics. With data-backed AI capabilities, hyper-automation can create a business process that interprets human language, comes up with the best business advice for the scenario, and then creates and analyses a series of steps, using bots to automate them. Hyper-automation aims to deliver the best business outcomes at the lowest cost while improving the accuracy and efficiency of business operations.

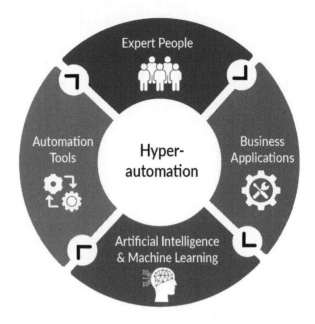

As a business owner, preparing for hyper-automation means focusing on upskilling your workforce to handle more strategic, creative and nonroutine tasks. While AI will automate a huge amount of the data processing and even data analysis, the goals must still be set by humans who understand the context, and the outcomes may also need to be sense-checked and delivered by employees. Hyper-automation requires a high level of planning and ongoing assessment to refine the models and outcomes, and employees will need to have the right expertise and capabilities to do this. For this to work, it's essential to establish a culture of change, preparing your employees for the evolving work environment.

Human-AI collaboration

This leads neatly to the trend I predict will dominate the future of the workforce – human–AI collaboration or 'augmented intelligence', where AI enhances human capabilities (as opposed to replacing them). AI will automate repetitive and mundane tasks, reducing errors and offering analytical insights, but human expertise, creativity and strategic thinking will remain indispensable. We're already seeing the use of AI (in particular, generative AI) supporting human learning, creativity and decision-making in a number of areas in society – from students planning, researching and compiling college essays through to judges weighing up legal arguments and handing down sentences.

Businesses should aim to create an environment that fosters this collaborative model. This requires striking the right balance between automation and human input, and creating an organisational culture that embraces technological advancements without sidelining the human element.

Ethical AI and regulatory frameworks

Alongside the excitement that's been generated by what AI can do, there is also a deep concern. As AI becomes more pervasive, issues around ethics and regulation will take centre stage, because while AI has shown the potential to have life-changing impact in areas such as healthcare and climate change, it has also shown a real potential for misuse: misuse of our personal data, the creation and spread of fake news, the use of deepfake technology for scams, and other actions that will damage individuals and society, such as the undermining of democracy and the corruption of the media.

All these issues, along with concerns about data privacy, algorithmic bias, transparency and accountability, will need to be addressed. We stand in a moment of history before the axe falls. We are on the cusp of technological breakthroughs that could solve some of the world's most pressing problems, but at the same time we are experiencing the fear that the same solution could destroy humankind or at least render it obsolete. We are about to open Pandora's jar, not knowing what might fly out. We are Prometheus, about to gift fire to our invention.

Unsurprisingly, the call for regulatory scrutiny and ethics guidelines has grown, and we're likely to see a considerable shift towards heavier regulation and guard rails for AI development and usage.

With tighter governance on the horizon, business owners would be well advised to prioritise ethical AI practices from the off. That means ensuring ML tools aren't being trained on copyrighted materials, and building in algorithmic transparency and data protection. It's also worth trying to stay informed about regulatory developments in the AI space and being prepared to adhere to any new guidelines or legislation.

The future is nearly here

AI is evolving and its refinement is happening fast. The future trends predicted here aren't going to occur somewhere down the road in five years' time. Innovations like Explainable AI (XAI), which will make AI decision-making processes more transparent, are already being actively developed. Advancements in areas like deep learning and neural networks, which will offer even more potential applications for businesses, are being reported on daily.

Staying on top of these trends is going to require a process of ongoing learning and an openness to innovation – which is one of the main reasons I suggest creating an innovation working group as part of your AI strategy.

Engaging with AI experts, tech consultants and even competitors while building in-house AI capabilities will help you to leverage these advancements. The future of AI in business is filled with potential. Understanding the trends and being strategic in your preparations and planning will enable you to ride the wave of AI evolution.

Maintaining your competitive edge

Staying current and competitive with AI will not only require an eye on the horizon for future trends, you'll also need a vision that extends beyond the initial stages I covered in earlier chapters. You'll need to build a long-term strategy around your AI goals to drive growth and efficiency through your innovation projects.

Creating a strategy for the long term depends on your specific business goals and goes beyond the scope of what I'm trying to do here in this book, but when you're thinking about a strategy that works for the long term, the principles I've gone over remain the same. Answer these seven questions:

1. **Do you have a clear vision for what you hope to achieve using AI?** Define your long-term aims and align them with your overall business strategy. You'll want to look at what's going on in your wider industry, what your competition is doing and what your customer expectations are, and use that knowledge as context for your goals.

2. **Do you have a group responsible for identifying AI opportunities in your company?** Having already run some AI initiatives, you'll have an idea of which areas create value for your business, but with AI developments coming thick and fast you'll want to ensure you have one eye

on the horizon so you can seize opportunities for strategic, high-value applications. Make space in your strategy for 'test and learn' projects so that you can stay on top of the latest AI trends.

3. **Do you have future-proof AI skills in strategic places across your organisation?** Embracing AI for the long term requires having great talent and may mean expanding your team to include data scientists, AI specialists, business analysts and project managers.

4. **Do you have confidence in the infrastructure you have in place for your data management and storage?** You'll have already begun putting together a storage and management solution, but for long-term success you'll need to consider your data privacy and security policies alongside how you collect and store data. Similarly, you'll need to make sure the IT infrastructure you have in place is robust enough to support the levels of AI deployment you're considering – whether that's on-site or cloud-based servers.

5. **Have you considered how to promote ethical and responsible AI in your organisation?** As you continue with your AI strategy for the longer term, it will be even more important to build trust with your stakeholders. It would be a good idea to have a code of conduct in place to consider the ethical implications within the different uses of AI across your business.

6. **Are your project management office and development teams set up for agile working?** Once you've run your pilot projects and had some quick wins, you need to think about scalability. The easiest way to expand the AI capabilities across your business while also adapting to shifting customer needs is by adopting agile methodologies. Agile working can help you to navigate change and uncertainty, working quicker and scaling more efficiently as a result.

7. **How are you measuring success?** I cannot overstate the importance of measurement. Using a framework like OKRs, as explained in Chapter Five, or by setting more traditional KPIs, you'll have a clearer idea of what's working and where ROI can be found. Regular monitoring and evaluation will keep you on track for the long term.

Maintaining a competitive edge is always a challenge, but using AI to its fullest and staying on track with it for the long term could be the best strategic approach for consistently staying ahead of the curve. As generative AI evolves, you'll be able to deliver even more personalised, seamless customer experiences, speeding up customer service with high-quality chatbots and lowering the cost of your marketing campaigns with AI-generated imagery, content and ads.

You'll access intel that will enable you to make smarter and more informed decisions, turning the data you collect from every area of your business into actionable insights and data-driven outcomes. AI is a prediction machine and the more you train it on your data the more accurate those predictions will be. Imagine what the impact of seeing the future could have on your business. Predicting market trends and customer behaviour could enable you to optimise every part of your operations. You'll have the ability to respond faster to changes in the market and in customer preferences. Pivoting depending on economic circumstances, as well as uncovering new revenue streams and opportunities, will help to safeguard your business from a turbulent marketplace and cast you as a market leader.

Preparing for disruptions

The past four years have seen levels of turbulence that no business expected and few were prepared for. Between the onset of the pandemic, supply chain breakdowns and economic volatility, some businesses have found it impossible to keep their heads above water, while others have adapted and thrived despite the instability of the marketplace. The majority, though, have found themselves somewhere in the middle – feeling the squeeze and trying to cut costs to get by.

The key to success in disruptive and unstable markets is resilience. Those who have adapted and survived are the ones with a clear resilience strategy in place to respond to changes and difficulties as they arise – and often before they arise, as they keep a vigilant watch on the horizon.

Resilience strategy

Business disruption is an absolute certainty for businesses that don't do resilience planning, but those that do will be able to turn disruption into opportunity. Their resilience strategy enables them to absorb stress, recover critical functionality and thrive in altered circumstances. External shock has a lesser impact on their operations and performance, and they can adapt and advance more quickly.

While resilience strategies vary massively depending on factors including organisational need, sector, size, region and more, using a simple framework can help businesses to define their starting point and work towards a long-term approach to resilience. My recommended framework is comprised of three phases based on sets of internal capabilities that create the foundation of a framework that will ensure lasting resilience and adaptability.

THE FUTURE OF AI IN ORGANISATIONS

Adapted from Teece & Linden, 2017[56]

Phase 1: Sensing is characterised as the ability to identify opportunities on the horizon and put people in place to observe trends and monitor uncertainties. In this first phase, companies develop the ability to sense changes. It consists of three subcategories: digital scouting, digital scenario planning and digital mindset crafting.

Phase 2: Seizing is characterised as the ability to reshape strategies and move quickly from assessment to action in response to the opportunities that arise. It means having people who experiment with innovative and entrepreneurial methods to build capabilities that strengthen agility for rapid responses to unexpected opportunities and threats. Phase 2 consists of three subcategories: strategic agility, rapid prototyping and balancing digital portfolios.

Phase 3: Transforming is characterised as the ability to deliver impact and lasting success, internally and externally, with operational certainty, and having engaged people and enabled leaders who have built a strong culture with a digital-first approach to challenges and creating new revenue streams. It consists of three micro-foundations: navigating innovation ecosystems, redesigning internal structures and improving digital maturity.

Companies require sensing capabilities to scan the external environment for unexpected trends that could disrupt the organisation. It's a scanning, creating, learning and interpreting activity that analyses diverse information about trends in the business ecosystem. It's a continuous process, which is why it should take place at all levels of the organisation. Frontline employees can help to provide information and insights into both external trends and internal inefficiencies to middle and top-level managers.[57]

Seizing capabilities enables companies to address opportunities or neutralise threats by experimenting with decentralised boundaries, digital platforms and new business models while ensuring leaders avoid hubris. Seizing is an experimental capability that supports action and commitment by using techniques such as rapid prototyping and real options logic to effectively balance risk and reward. Agile working methods have been particularly impactful in this phase, helping organisations to seize opportunities in an iterative manner where they don't have the confidence or ability to adjust entire business models for radical innovation.

Both of these phases act as a foundation to the final step. Sensing and seizing capabilities helps create and discover opportunities, but to execute an AI strategy, firms need transforming capabilities to realise the full potential of strategic change. This means adopting an entrepreneurial, agile mindset, actively cultivating innovation and taking an innovative approach to problem-solving and a broad expansive approach to external network building. Moving from sensing and seizing capabilities to developing transforming capabilities supports companies with the strategic renewal of their assets and structures, enabling them to respond to ever-evolving environments.

Building these capabilities and moving through these three phases will improve your organisational resilience and resilience-building skills. It will help you to create a long-term resilience strategy that designs, creates and refines a defensible business model, guides transformation and provides a resilient foundation for future issues and a durable source for obtaining competitive advantage.

Summary

Chapter Seven is an exploration of the future of AI. I discussed the likely future trends, such as the democratisation of AI and ethical and regulatory frameworks, before moving on to discuss how to use AI to maintain a competitive edge with a robust long-term strategy. I posed seven critical questions to help you evaluate the longevity of your strategy, starting with your vision and ending with your measurement. Finally, I covered long-term resilience and the three rungs on the ladder to achieve this: the ability to sense AI developments on the horizon, seize AI opportunities as they present themselves, and transform your company through AI.

Conclusion

It's been a whistle-stop tour, but I've taken you through the key components of successfully transforming your organisation with AI. I've helped you to assess your preparedness to implement AI and walked you through the process of creating your own roadmap. I've taken a brief look into the near future to give you an idea of what you may need to prepare for. What should by now be clear is that AI presents a host of opportunities to streamline your business operations, reduce costs and identify new revenue streams.

The implications of AI could be transformational for your business. Whether it's automation, data analysis, personalisation, customer support, product innovation or supply chain optimisation, there are opportunities for every business to capitalise on. The crucial components for doing so are:

- Your leadership team
- Your internal talent
- Your company culture

Addressing these three areas in readiness for building an AI strategy will improve your chances of success by over 50%.

That means getting early buy-in; getting the right stakeholders in the right places and making them champions for your AI initiatives; upskilling, redeploying and hiring talent with the right expertise; breaking down silos and encouraging collaborative working; and increasing transparency and trust across the workforce to remove fear triggers around using AI and job losses. The result will be huge productivity gains, increased resilience in a fast-moving market, an improved CVP and new revenue streams for your company.

Recap of key takeaways

What is most apparent from the past twelve months is that it's no longer a matter of *if*, it's a matter of *when*. AI is a reality that will reshape the entire marketplace. Business leaders who choose to bury their heads in the sand and attempt to ignore the available

CONCLUSION

tools will be outpaced by competitors who embrace them. I've given you a number of examples of using AI across different industries, and looked at case studies that show the incredible value that AI has already had for those organisations using it well, but for those wanting to realise the full, long-term potential that AI holds, there is more to it than picking a tool and telling people to use it.

I've explored a process for assessing your business readiness for AI, one that:

- Prioritises agility as a way of working to ensure speed and scale
- Builds trust as a cornerstone of your relationship with your employees and customers
- Centres your projects around customer ease and experience
- Encourages and rewards innovation at every level of your organisation

Once you've laid your foundations – having a vision and the ability to communicate that vision, assessing the risks, embedding agile methodologies and putting the right talent in place – you can create a roadmap for implementing AI.

Across these chapters I've aimed to give you a blueprint to help you adapt your organisation's strategy and structure to constantly capture opportunities enabled by AI in a timely manner. You don't have to be the next Uber or have the next AI discovery. If you are aiming to achieve better and more efficient frontline customer service, and this only requires the use of a new spreadsheet, if it makes business sense, you are capturing an opportunity. Then it's simply a case of starting with the first one and building on that success to go after the next. Over time, you'll develop your sense of where to look and how to capture what you're looking for.

By reading this book, you are starting a process of change. Following the structure I've laid out here, your roadmap should consist of the following five simple steps:

1. **Identify the challenge:** This is where you discover where the opportunities lie. To do this, you need to understand the value that can be unlocked from your business. You can use AI to provide the catalyst in the form of objective, evidence-based data analysis and insights. These insights can be found from technology trends, market conditions, financial results, customer satisfaction surveys or any other source of data representative of the environment.

2. **Frame the challenge:** Once you've worked out where you can extract value, you need to give people a purpose, something to work towards; you need to frame the challenge as something that those people who need to change care about.

This could be something as general as growing the business, delighting customers or being the best place to work. Once you have a goal, you then need to put a framework, like OKRs, in place to help those same people track their progress towards that goal.

In doing this, not only will you motivate people but you will allow them room to make their own meaning, to take the initiative and experiment. In turn, this will lead to greater buy-in, a sense of ownership and more innovation. It will avoid misinterpretation of the vision, which might lead to 'declaring the victory too soon', a leading factor of failures in change initiatives.[58] The picture of the future you paint should motivate enough people who need to change to make that change willingly and of their own volition.

3. **Engage stakeholders:** This is where you find a shared understanding and alignment at the outset of your AI project. This means aligning the perspectives of your stakeholders, engaging them and enabling them to take action. You'll identify the stakeholders who are required to make the change, impacted by the change or sponsoring the change, and work with them to develop use cases.

These will be leaders and senior managers who have visibility of the areas where AI could have significant benefit. They will help to identify quick wins to begin with and future opportunities as they arise.

4. **Bring it to life:** Never has a revolution been started by citing best practice: it doesn't work for the most part and it certainly doesn't motivate. Change is contextual and people are motivated by understanding how it affects them personally. Prototyping gives people the opportunity to find answers to key questions like 'What's in it for me?', 'How will it impact me?' and 'Where do I fit in?'

5. **Evaluate:** With OKRs in place, evaluation also needs to be a constant part of the project scope. Regular, set retrospectives will help assess progress towards milestones and overall goals. Having regular touchpoints for monitoring the progress of a project and measuring its relative success will ensure timely course correction, a quicker response to external changes and the ability to link work with business successes. This will help to keep morale and momentum high and make it easier to make the case for larger and more complex AI projects.

Final thoughts on embracing AI for competitive advantage

You should now feel equipped with the tools to assess your readiness and create your own roadmap for AI. Before you begin planning your journey, here are a

CONCLUSION

few final thoughts on how to ensure your AI projects are a success and don't fall foul of the most common mistakes I see companies make.

Allocate a budget

Nothing derails a digital project more quickly than running out of money halfway through or cutting corners en route to the finish line. Make sure you have enough funding to reach your goals before you start your project. This means identifying and understanding the core business priorities you'll address with AI. It also means examining the strategies involved and allocating budgets from relevant departments accordingly. As a rule, overestimate – keep headroom for adjustments based on ROI. If something unexpected works well, you want the reserves available to scale it.

Top-down

One of the main reasons AI projects fail is lack of vision and leadership at the top. As already mentioned, having an engaged CEO and board-level support is crucial. Becoming a company that is oriented around AI will likely require a significant culture change. This change needs to be modelled at the top.

Having an open-minded leadership team who are open to experimentation and allow their teams to try and to fail will create a culture of innovation.

Before a company embraces digital and AI, company leaders need to become digital leaders who think 'end to end' about how they can use AI to produce a step change in both performance and value for their customers.

There are certain behaviours that leaders can cultivate to do this: developing a mindset of curiosity, asking why rather than saying no, anticipating objections and addressing them early, simplifying processes and decision-making so that momentum isn't lost, and being open about mistakes and removing blame culture to enable others to make and learn from their mistakes too.

Unlock creativity through diversity

I've talked a lot about talent in the earlier chapters of this book; in particular, cultivating the right skills across your organisation to get your AI projects off the ground. Another key factor is the diversity of your people. Greater diversity unlocks huge potential for creativity.

Inclusive companies are 1.7 times more likely to be market leaders in innovation.[59] According to Harvard Business Review, the innovation revenue in companies with above-average total diversity was 19% points higher.[60] In addition, employees in a company with higher workplace diversity have access to a variety of different perspectives, and research shows diverse leadership teams who listen to a range of voices make better business decisions up to 87% of the time.[61]

In short, not only will you benefit from more innovation, but your team will likely make more profitable decisions, which will further increase your competitive advantage.

Go on your own journey

The temptation is to choose your AI projects based on what your competitors are doing, investing in the same areas and comparing outcomes, but you're more likely to see long-term success if you use AI to enhance your unique advantages. This is one of the reasons I advise that your AI projects are intrinsically linked to your business plan: it is far better to set your business goals, focus on what makes your organisation different and create an integrated strategy for introducing AI into your business. Base this strategy on internal feedback from those departments that will interact with AI, and you are far more likely to succeed than by attempting to replicate a competitor.

Similarly, it's important not to focus overly on comparing your timescales with those of your competitor. While it makes sense to have an eye on your competition, don't be distracted and don't rush projects to keep up with the timescales of others.

External help

My research suggests that the two main blockers for AI implementation are having the skill set internally to run the projects, and the complexity of the solutions and tech available. One of the quickest ways to resolve both is to bring in external help from digital consultancies with experience of the tools and the contexts in which they'll be used.

Whether you're ready for it or not, the age of AI is upon us. To be a player in this new economy, and to keep pace with consumers' ever-increasing expectations, you will have to think carefully about how you're going to respond to it and to the new tech available. One thing is certain: ignoring this new way of doing business won't be an option for long. While there are concerns around the current trustworthiness of generative AI, the accuracy of predictive AI is improving every day. Concerns around data privacy and governance are being answered.

Making a leap into a new way of doing business is not something to be taken lightly, but these chapters have provided you with convincing use cases and tools to bolster your confidence. If you take one thing away with you, it should be the understanding that AI isn't a destination for businesses, it's an ever-evolving tool you can wield to help you reach your goals faster and with more precision. Just as a tool cannot be of use without a craftsman's hand, AI requires capable, talented people to develop, train and use it for it to add maximum value. AI is a tool to enhance the skills and improve the systems you already have available to you. Rather than offer a discussion about AI replacing human ability, this book is the catalyst for you to embark on your journey towards amplified intelligence, complementing and extending what you have already built.

Summary

I've rounded up the crucial components and key takeaways of the book, giving you a five-step process to follow to build your own roadmap. I've concluded with some final advice – the key points that are crucial to success but are often overlooked in companies that embark on these large, transformational projects.

Across the course of this book, I have aimed to strike a balance between laying the technical and theoretical groundwork needed before you embark on your AI transformations, and giving you the practical guidance and strategic input to help you assess your readiness for your AI journey. I have set out concrete steps to follow to create a roadmap that will lead you to success.

This book is a tool that enables you to do four things: understand what AI is and what it can do, identify where AI will have the greatest impact in your business, assess your business readiness for AI initiatives, and carve out your roadmap for AI. If it goes some way towards giving you the confidence to move forward and become more equipped for the needs and priorities of your customers, then I'll view it as a success.

Notes

1. S K Tran, 'GOOGLE: A reflection of culture, leader, and management', *International Journal of Corporate Social Responsibility* (19 December 2017), https://doi.org/10.1186/s40991-017-0021-0, accessed 30 October 2023
2. S A Hewlett, et al, 'How Diversity Can Drive Innovation', *Harvard Business Review* (December 2013), https://hbr.org/2013/12/how-diversity-can-drive-innovation, accessed 30 October 2023
3. Forbes Insights, 'Global Diversity and Inclusion: Fostering innovation through a diverse workforce', *Forbes* (no date), https://images.forbes.com/forbesinsights/StudyPDFs/Innovation_Through_Diversity.pdf, accessed 30 October 2023
4. Forbes LinkedIn, 'Steve Forbes Speaks At Yass Prize Semi-Finalist Announcement', *Forbes* (5 October 2022), www.linkedin.com/posts/forbes-magazine_steve-forbes-speaks-at-yass-prize-semi-finalist-activity-6986436239608442881-UVeh/, accessed 6 November 2023
5. S Keller, 'Attracting and Retaining the Right Talent', McKinsey & Company (24 November 2017), www.mckinsey.com/capabilities/people-and-organizational-performance/our-insights/attracting-and-retaining-the-right-talent, accessed 30 October 2023

6   ibid
7   World Economic Forum, 'Recession and Automation Changes Our Future of Work, But There are Jobs Coming, Report Says' (20 October 2020), www.weforum.org/press/2020/10/recession-and-automation-changes-our-future-of-work-but-there-are-jobs-coming-report-says-52c5162fce/, accessed 30 October 2023
8   LinkedIn, 'Future of Work Report: AI at Work' (August 2023), https://economicgraph.linkedin.com/content/dam/me/economicgraph/en-us/PDF/future-of-work-report-ai-august-2023.pdf, accessed 30 October 2023
9   Microsoft, '2023 Work Trend Index Annual Report: Will AI Fix Work?' (9 May 2023), https://assets.ctfassets.net/y8fb0rhks3b3/5eyZc6gDu1bzftdY6w3ZVV/edddc40a33f7e78b3d55a64b590825ac/WTI_Will_AI_Fix_Work_051723.pdf, accessed 30 October 2023
10 'Future of Jobs Report 2023', World Economic Forum (May 2023), www3.weforum.org/docs/WEF_Future_of_Jobs_2023.pdf, accessed 6 November 2023
11 M Chui et al, 'Notes from the AI frontier: Applications and value of deep learning', McKinsey & Company (17 April 2018), www.mckinsey.com/featured-insights/artificial-intelligence/notes-from-the-ai-frontier-applications-and-value-of-deep-learning, accessed 30 October 2023
12 Deloitte Insights, 'Becoming an AI-fueled organization' (no date), www2.deloitte.com/us/en/insights/focus/cognitive-technologies/state-of-ai-and-intelligent-automation-in-business-survey.html, accessed 30 October 2023
13 S Taufik, 'Generative AI to reach $1.3t in revenue by 2032: Bloomberg Intelligence', Tech In Asia (9 June 2023), www.techinasia.com/generative-ai-to-reach-1-3t-in-revenue-by-2032-bloomberg-intelligence, accessed 30 October 2023
14 M Alam and A ur R Khokhar, 'Impact of the Internet on Customer Loyalty in Swedish Banks', Luleå University of Technology (16 March 2006), www.diva-portal.org/smash/get/diva2:1021675/FULLTEXT01.pdf, accessed 30 October 2023
15 H Kiros, 'Doctors using AI catch breast cancer more often than either does alone', *MIT Technology Review* (11/07/2022), www.technologyreview.com/2022/07/11/1055677/ai-diagnose-breast-cancer-mammograms, accessed 12 June 2023
16 CAU Hassan et al, 'Effectively Predicting the Presence of Coronary Heart Disease Using Machine Learning

Classifiers', *Sensors (Basel)*, 22(19):7227 (23 Sep 2022), https://pubmed.ncbi.nlm.nih.gov/36236325, accessed 2 October 2023

17 ImproveWell, 'How Royal Cornwall Hospitals NHS Trust is using ImproveWell to make lasting change' (2019), www.improvewell.com/blog/royal-cornwall-nhs-lasting-change, accessed 3 July 2023

18 F Savage, *Chatbots: Market forecasts, sector analysis and future strategies 2023–2028* (Juniper Research, 2023), www.juniperresearch.com/researchstore/operators-providers/chatbots-trends-research-report, accessed 2 October 2023

19 ibid

20 S Biswas et al, *Building the AI bank of the future* (McKinsey & Company, 2021), www.mckinsey.com/industries/financial-services/our-insights/introduction-building-the-ai-bank-of-the-future, accessed 19 June 2023

21 OP Schleichert et al, *Predictive Maintenance: Taking proactive measures based on advanced data analytics to predict and avoid machine failure* (Deloitte, 2017), www2.deloitte.com/content/dam/Deloitte/de/Documents/deloitte-analytics/Deloitte_Predictive-Maintenance_PositionPaper.pdf, accessed 2 October 2023

22 H Bauer at al, *Smartening Up with Artificial Intelligence (AI) – What's in it for Germany and its industrial sector?* (McKinsey & Company, 2017), www.mckinsey.com/industries/semiconductors/our-insights/smartening-up-with-artificial-intelligence, accessed 2 October 2023

23 L Rainie et al, 'How Americans think about artificial intelligence', Pew Research Center (17 March 2022), www.pewresearch.org/internet/2022/03/17/how-americans-think-about-artificial-intelligence/, accessed 30 October 2023

24 V Beauchene et al, 'AI at Work: What people are saying', BCG (7 June 2023), www.bcg.com/publications/2023/what-people-are-saying-about-ai-at-work, accessed 30 October 2023

25 E Baptista, 'China uses AI software to improve its surveillance capabilities' (Reuters, 2022), www.reuters.com/world/china/china-uses-ai-software-improve-its-surveillance-capabilities-2022-04-08, accessed 12 June 2023

26 A Persson et al, *We Mostly Think Alike: Individual differences in attitude towards AI in Sweden and Japan, The Review of*

Socionetwork Strategies, 15 (2021), 123–142, https://doi.org/10.1007/s12626-021-00071-y

27 Statista, 'Spending on digital transformation technologies and services worldwide from 2017 to 2026' (2022), www.statista.com/statistics/870924/worldwide-digital-transformation-market-size, accessed 2 October 2023

28 M Bucey et al, 'The "how" of transformation' (McKinsey & Company, 9 May 2016), www.mckinsey.com/industries/retail/our-insights/the-how-of-transformation, accessed 15 March 2023

29 ibid

30 C Dilmegani, '85+ Digital Transformation Stats from Reputable Sources, (AIMultiple, 5 December 2022), https://research.aimultiple.com/digital-transformation-stats, accessed 20 March 2023

31 J Derksen, 'Breaking Down Internal Barriers in Companies Crucial Amid Increasing Digitization, Accenture Study Finds', Accenture (2020), https://newsroom.accenture.com/news/2020/breaking-down-internal-barriers-in-companies-crucial-amid-increasing-digitization-accenture-study-finds, accessed 20 December 2023

32 P Daugherty et al, 'A new era of generative AI for everyone', Accenture (2023), www.accenture.com/content/dam/accenture/final/accenture-com/document/Accenture-A-New-Era-of-Generative-AI-for-Everyone.pdf, accessed 6 November 2023

33 S Keller et al, 'Losing from day one: Why even successful transformations fall short' (McKinsey & Company, 2021), www.mckinsey.com/capabilities/people-and-organizational-performance/our-insights/successful-transformations, accessed 2 October 2023

34 R Knaster, *15th State of Agile Report: Agile leads the way through the pandemic and digital transformation* (digital.ai, 2021), https://digital.ai/catalyst-blog/15th-state-of-agile-report-agile-leads-the-way-through-the-pandemic-and-digital, accessed 12 November 2022

35 You can learn more about the Agile principles from a number of sources, including Agile Alliance: www.agilealliance.org/agile101/12-principles-behind-the-agile-manifesto/, accessed 12 October 2023

36 BCG, 'Companies Can Flip the Odds of Success in Digital Transformations from 30% to 80%' (29 October 2020), www.bcg.com/press/29october2020-companies-can-flip-the-

NOTES

odds-of-success-in-digital-transformations-from-30-to-80, accessed 30 October 2023

37 J Woodcock and M Graham, *The Gig Economy: A Critical Introduction* (Polity, 2019)

38 CIPD, 'Flexible Working: A step to creating more inclusive workplaces' (26 September 2019), www.cipd.org/uk/about/news/flexible-working, accessed 30 October 2023

39 L Rainie et al, 'How Americans think about artificial intelligence' (Pew Research Center, 2022), www.pewresearch.org/internet/2022/03/17/how-americans-think-about-artificial-intelligence, accessed 17 April 2023

40 GOV.UK, 'Cyber Security Breaches Survey 2022', www.gov.uk/government/statistics/cyber-security-breaches-survey-2022/cyber-security-breaches-survey-2022, accessed 27 March 2023

41 J Dastin, 'Amazon scraps secret AI recruiting tool that showed bias against women', Reuters (11 October 2018), www.reuters.com/article/us-amazon-com-jobs-automation-insight-idUSKCN1MK08G, accessed 30 October 2023

42 M Gentzel, 'Biased Face Recognition Technology Used by Government: A Problem for Liberal Democracy', *Springer Nature* (25 September 2021), www.ncbi.nlm.nih.gov/pmc/articles/PMC8475322, accessed 30 October 2023

43 J Turner, '7 Technology Disruptions That Will Completely Change Sales', Gartner (10 October 2022), www.gartner.com/en/articles/7-technology-disruptions-that-will-completely-change-sales, accessed 30 October 2023

44 P Forth et al, *Flipping the Odds of Digital Transformation Success* (Boston Consulting Group, October 2020), accessed 15 May 2023

45 ibid

46 ibid

47 ibid

48 S Zuboff, *The Age of Surveillance Capitalism: The fight for a human future at the new frontier of power* (Profile Books, 2019)

49 L Andrews, 'A new privacy paradigm in the age of apps', *Wake Forest Law Review*, 53/3 (2018) 421–477

50 B Kahraman, 'Complementarities and Concerns', Presentation: Module 2: The Business of Big Data and Machine Learning, 5 2023

51 S Coyne et al, 'Does time spent using social media impact mental health?: An eight year longitudinal study',

Computers in Human Behavior, 104 (March 2020), https://doi.org/10.1016/j.chb.2019.106160

52 HE Aldrich, *Organizations and Environments* (Stanford University Press, 2008); M Zollo and S Winter, 'Deliberate learning and the evolution of dynamic capabilities', *Organization Science*, 13/3 (2002) 339–51

53 Appen, *The 2020 State of AI and Machine Learning Report* (2019), https://appen.com/whitepapers/the-state-of-ai-and-machine-learning-report, accessed 17 April 2023

54 K Weller, 'Social Media as a Source for Research Data', Workshop at National Centre for Research Methods (July 2016), www.ncrm.ac.uk/training/show.php?article=6451, accessed 5 June 2023

55 DataRobot, *State of AI Bias* (2022), www.datarobot.com/wp-content/uploads/2022/01/DataRobot-Report-State-of-AI-Bias_V5.pdf, accessed 16 May 2023

56 DJ Teece and G Linden, 'Business models, value capture, and the digital enterprise', *Journal of Organization Design*, 6/1 (24 August 2017) 1–14, https://link.springer.com/article/10.1186/s41469-017-0018-x, accessed 2 October 2023

57 ibid

58 J P Kotter, 'Leading Change: Why Transformation Efforts Fail', *Harvard Business Review* (May 1995), https://hbr.org/1995/05/leading-change-why-transformation-efforts-fail-2, accessed 30 October 2023

59 J Bersin, 'Why Diversity and Inclusion Has Become a Business Priority' (7 December 2015, updated 16 March 2019), https://joshbersin.com/2015/12/why-diversity-and-inclusion-will-be-a-top-priority-for-2016/, accessed 30 October 2023

60 R Lorenzo and M Reeves, 'How and Where Diversity Drives Financial Performance', *Harvard Business Review* (2018), https://hbr.org/2018/01/how-and-where-diversity-drives-financial-performance, accessed 15 May 2023

61 A Stahl, '3 Benefits of Diversity in the Workplace' (Forbes, 2021), www.forbes.com/sites/ashleystahl/2021/12/17/3-benefits-of-diversity-in-the-workplace/?sh=18eed24422ed, accessed 5 June 2023

Acknowledgements

To my grandparents, who instilled in me the value of pragmatism and the discipline of first-principle thinking.

To my wife for her unending support and for taking on the mental load, enabling me to focus.

To my children, whose admiration for me is motivational and who inspire me daily with their curiosity.

To the numerous mentors whose wisdom and feedback have shaped my thinking and career.

To everyone who believed in me.

The Author

Peter Verster is an entrepreneurial leader with solid academic foundations earned at Saïd Business School, University of Oxford. This forms the groundwork upon which he has built a successful career with a documented track record of organisational transformation across global enterprises, including Microsoft, Adidas, Tesco and AstraZeneca.

South African born and bred, his direct, pragmatic and hands on style has earned him the respect of leaders in some of the world's largest organisations, where he has applied his laser focus on using data and AI to drive business value and foster innovation. Peter's wealth of knowledge and experience provides a unique opportunity to be guided by an expert in solving real world problems using data and AI, which has been the hallmark of his career and the bedrock for this book.

Peter lives in Cheshire, England, with his wife and two daughters, loves golf and thrives at the intersection of technology and business.

🌐 peterverster.com